Hitler's Wolfsschanze

Hitler's Wolfsschanze

The Wolf's Lair Headquarters on the Eastern Front – An Illustrated Guide

John Grehan

AN IMPRINT OF PEN & SWORD BOOKS LTD
YORKSHIRE – PHILADELPHIA

First published in Great Britain in 2021 by
FRONTLINE BOOKS
an imprint of Pen & Sword Books Ltd
47 Church Street, Barnsley, S. Yorkshire, S70 2AS

ISBN: 978-1-52675-311-3

CIP data records for this title are available from the British Library.

For more information on our books, please visit www.frontline-books.com, email info@frontline-books.com or write to us at the above address.

Typeset by Concept, Huddersfield, West Yorkshire, HD4 5JL
Printed and bound in India by Replika Press Pvt. Ltd.

FSC www.fsc.org MIX Paper from responsible sources FSC® C016779

Pen & Sword Books Ltd incorporates the imprints of Pen & Sword Archaeology, Atlas, Aviation, Battleground, Discovery, Family History, History, Maritime, Military, Naval, Politics, Social History, Transport, True Crime, Claymore Press, Frontline Books, Praetorian Press, Seaforth Publishing and White Owl.

For a complete list of Pen & Sword titles please contact
PEN & SWORD LTD
47 Church Street, Barnsley, South Yorkshire, S70 2AS, England
E-mail: enquiries@pen-and-sword.co.uk
or
PEN & SWORD BOOKS
1950 Lawrence Rd, Havertown, PA 19083, USA
E-mail: Uspen-and-sword@casematepublishers.com

Contents

Foreword

Hitler's Wolf's Lair was (and is) one of the most sinister Second World War sites. From there, he commanded the German armed forces in his attack on Soviet Russia. Hitler controlled all phases of the war in Russia from the Wolf's Lair from June 1941 to November 1944 (except for a period in 1942 when Hitler stayed at a field headquarters in the Ukraine), until the site was blown up to prevent capture by the rapidly advancing Russians in January 1945.

The Wolf's Lair became the most famous of Hitler's *Führerhauptquartier* (field headquarters). During the war it was a closely guarded secret, hidden deep in the woods in a remote part of East Prussia. Hitler demanded the ruthless conquest of Russia and pitiless reprisals against partisans while he was in the Wolf's Lair, and it was there that Colonel Stauffenberg and the German resistance tried to assassinate him with a bomb in July 1944. In all, Hitler spent over 800 days at the Wolf's Lair, directing his war on the Eastern Front.

John Grehan's book details not only the layout and appearance of the Wolf's Lair, but also stories of daily life there such as bathing in the nearby lakes and the battles against the ever-present mosquitoes. Additionally, the book covers other associated nearby headquarters such as the Wehrmacht High Command headquarters at Mauerwald, Himmler's bunker at Hochwald, Göring's *Robinson* headquarters, and others.

The layout of the Wolf's Lair and other headquarters is well described, showing the different buildings and bunkers, explaining how these headquarters sites were planned and built, with plentiful period and modern photographs to illustrate the text.

Stauffenberg's assassination attempt gets a chapter to itself, and it reads like a mystery novel. All the details are here – the elaborate plans of the resistance members, previous attempts that went awry, Stauffenberg's plans and actions on 20 July 1944 at the Wolf's Lair, his route to escape the scene of the assassination attempt, and the aftermath at the Wolf's Lair and in Berlin.

When the bunkers and buildings were blown up in January 1945, the Wolf's Lair was abandoned for many years, but the Polish authorities have now opened the area up for tourists, who are well-rewarded by a walk along the many marked paths, among the ruined buildings and destroyed bunkers of a site that played an important part in the history of the Second World War.

Geoff Walden
The Third Reich in Ruins

A Cautionary Note

Anyone who should wish to visit any of the headquarters sites described in this book should be aware that, just as in the 1940s, mosquitoes inhabit every bunker and every path. These are seriously aggressive creatures whose proboscis can even penetrate thin clothing and are at their most aggressive during the summer months. Some indication of their relentless pursuit of human blood can be gauged by an event that took place one day at the *Wolfsschanze*, as related by one of Hitler's bodyguards, Rochus Misch of the RSD: 'Less pleasant experiences were had with the mosquitoes. They plagued us and bothered us endlessly. Without the nets which covered our heads, we would have been eaten alive. For one of our colleagues, the mosquitoes provided quite another unexpected consequence. Adjutant Fritz Darges, previously adjutant to Martin Bormann, was standing one day with his hands in his trouser pockets close to Hitler awaiting his orders. I was not far away and saw Hitler leafing through a batch of papers. Suddenly a mosquito began buzzing about Hitler's head. Heavy-handed and angry, Hitler hit out at the mosquito with the paperwork but without the desired result. The accursed thing was appeared quite unimpressed, and after the wild gesticulations had ended, would always settle again on exactly the same spot from where Hitler had attempted to shoo it away. Fritz could hardly conceal his laughter at the Führer being second best in an aerial dogfight with a mosquito. Fritz had not moved a centimetre from where he was; his hands were still in his pockets, and he was grinning. This was not overlooked by Hitler, even in his excitement. He looked at Fritz sharply: 'If you are not even able to keep a thing like that off my body, then you have no business being here!' Fritz understood at once and went off to pack his trunk. The same evening, he was on his way to the front.'

Take heavy, long-sleeved tops, do not wear shorts, wear headgear, and apply copious and frequent applications of insect repellent. You have been warned!

Chapter 1

Führerhauptquartiere Wolfsschanze

The German invasion of the Soviet Union on 22 June 1941 shocked the world; it was though, hardly a surprise. Hitler had made his intentions quite clear many years earlier. After his failed coup in 1923, he had been incarcerated in Landsberg Prison, where he began work on his quasi-autobiographical book, *Mein Kampf*, in which he set out his political ideology and his future hopes for Germany. In this he wrote, with reference to the First World War: 'If new territory were to be acquired in Europe it must have been mainly at Russia's cost, and once again the new German Empire should have set out on its march along the same road as was formerly trodden by the Teutonic Knights, this time to acquire soil for the German plough by means of the German sword and thus provide the nation with its daily bread.'

Hitler was fixated with the acquisition of more territory for the expanding German nation – the infamous *Lebensraum*, or living space – and he made it quite clear where that living space would be found: 'We shall soon reach a point beyond which the resources of our soil can no longer be exploited,' he wrote, 'and at the same time we shall reach a point beyond which our man-power cannot develop ... If we speak of soil in Europe today, we can primarily have in mind only Russia and her vassal border states.'

Remarkably, he was able to find a justification for seizing Russian territory: 'One must calmly and squarely face the truth that it certainly cannot be part of the dispensation of Divine Providence to give a fifty times larger share of the soil of this world to one nation than to another. In considering this state of affairs to-day, one must not allow existing political frontiers to distract attention from what ought to exist on principles of strict justice. If this earth has sufficient room for all, then we ought to have that share of the soil which is absolutely necessary for our existence.'

Having stated his beliefs in this fashion and repeated such philosophies many times during the intervening years, Hitler felt impelled to fulfil these promises to his people. He would give them their *Lebensraum* and would clear the Slavs from the territory he won – and it would be won by the sword. Few then, could have doubted that at some point, Germany would invade the Soviet Union.

However, one day in 1941, while sitting in the *Führerbunker* in the *Wolfsschanze* alone with his friend and photographer, Heinrich Hoffmann, Hitler gave quite a different explanation for the attack upon the Soviet Union:

'Through a concatenation of circumstances, I was compelled to take the first step in what is a war of prevention – and let me emphasise, it must be explained with the utmost clarity to the German people, that is indeed a war of prevention. It was vital that I get my blow in first, before the Russians struck ... We need oil for our aircraft, oil for our armour, and the thrust towards the Russian oilfields must at all costs succeed.'[1]

Hitler's first step eastward was taken on 1 September 1939, when he invaded Poland. Stalin and his acolytes had been duped into a pact with Germany that enabled the Führer to attack Poland knowing that the Soviets would join him in occupying and partitioning the country. When the subjugation of Poland had been accomplished, German and Soviet forces faced each other across the agreed demarcation line. While Stalin believed that Hitler had achieved his ends and that he would honour the terms of the Molotov–Ribbentrop Pact, Hitler was planning the invasion of Russia.

In the autumn of 1940, Dr Fritz Todt, a construction engineer who had formed a civil and military engineering organisation, Organisation Todt (OT), and who in March of that year had been made Reich Minister for Armaments and Ammunition, was instructed to find a suitable site for the establishment of a headquarters complex close to the border with the Soviets from where the Führer and his staff could direct the assault upon the USSR.

Todt set off for East Prussia, taking with him his army adjutant, Hauptmann (later Generalleutnant) Gerhard Engel, and other headquarters staff and construction specialists. After a prolonged search, a site was found deep inside the forest of Görlitz, 5 miles to the east of the town of Rastenburg, which is today's Polish town of Kętrzyn, and 50 miles from the Soviet border. There would be built the largest of all the Führer headquarters (*Führerhauptquartiere*), which during its secret construction was called the *Chemische Werke Askania* (Askania Chemical Works) or *Anlage Nord* (Camp, or installation or facility, North) but would soon be known as the *Wolfsschanze* – the Wolf's Lair.

There were a number of reasons why the Görlitz forest was chosen by Todt. To the east is the great Mazurian Lakes system, which forms a 70km-long natural water obstacle against ground-based troops. Also to the east, between two of the larger lakes, is the Boyen fortress (more of which in a later chapter) which was situated in an important strategic position and had played a part in the momentous Battle of Tannenberg against the Russians in the First World War. There were also barracks and garrison towns in the general vicinity. One-third of the area was woodland and it was only sparsely populated, both of which helped with security and concealment.

The need for a static base close to the centre of operations had become clear during the invasion of Poland in 1939. Before the outbreak of hostilities, no measures had been taken to establish a forward command post for the war for either Hitler or the High Command of the Armed Forces, the *Oberkommando der Wehrmacht* (OKW). This meant that the leadership travelled around on Hitler's special command train, the *Führersonderzug Amerika*, while the senior staff of the army, the Heer, and the air force, the Luftwaffe, were sitting in their own respective headquarters. Clearly, this was an unsatisfactory arrangement.

Though Hitler had been persuaded to establish a settled base for the invasion of France and the Low Countries in May 1940, the first of the static *Führerhauptquartiere*, the *Felsennest* (Rocky Nest), was small and cramped, with just four rooms. It would be quite different for the campaign in the East. The *Wolfsschanze* and the corresponding Army headquarters at nearby *Mauerwald* would be largest and most complex of all the command installations. During the war, 12.9 million working days, each lasting between eight and sixteen hours, were spent on building the various *Führerhauptquartiere* across Europe. The workforce reached 1.5 million as the war progressed.

Hitler officially ordered the construction of the *Wolfsschanze* and *Mauerwald* on 15 November 1940, with the instruction that the work had to be complete by the following April. Work soon began on the *Wolfsschanze*. The forest was cleared of inhabitants and buildings and a forbidden zone with a radius of 10km extended around the site surrounded by barbed wire and fences, and the road from Rastenburg was given a new asphalt surface. Outside and inside the main perimeter fence were infantry trenches, dugouts, munitions depots and wooden barracks for the guards and a fire brigade crew. Inside the fence there was also a minefield approximately 150m wide as well as camouflaged watch towers that stood up to 35m high. At each entrance to the *Wolfsschanze* was a barrier, on both sides of which were displayed signs that read, 'Stop Military Object. No Admittance to Civilians'. Once permitted through the barriers, which were guarded night and day, other signs warned visitors: 'It is forbidden to leave this road. Danger to Life. Commanding Officer'. Similar signs were placed all around the perimeter.

The use of the Askania Chemical Works as a 'front' enabled the legitimate purchase of materials from unsuspecting contractors. These included the firm Hoyer from Hamburg, which produced monolithic reinforced concrete structures; the Draiger (or Draeger) company, which dealt with ventilation and filtering systems; Klaus Ackermann, which made reinforced concrete blocks; and the company Warenvertrieb GmbH, which dealt with barracks, warehouses and service structures.

Thousands of construction workers of the Organisation Todt and the *Hochtief Aktiengesellschaft* were transported into the area under the auspices of the *Konstrukionsburo*.[2] The companies Wayss & Freytag and Dyckerhoff & Widmann, which specialised in bunker construction, acted as general contractors for the construction work. All the workers all wore greenish-brown uniforms that had been taken from the Czech army in 1939 following the German invasion of that country.

The former Hindenburg Barracks at Rastenburg.

The area around Rastenburg was soon populated by work detachments, with some of the workers being accommodated in the town itself and in the local Hindenburg Army barracks. The Organisation Todt also had a building materials warehouse at Rastenburg train station as well as a food depot at the Rastenburg Sugar Factory.

Just how many people were employed on the building work on the Wolf's Lair is not known with any degree of certainty and figures from 2,000 to more than 5,000 have been suggested. These workers were repeatedly checked for security concerns by officials of the *Reichssicherheitsdienst* (RSD), the Reich Security Service, and the construction sites and material stores were guarded by soldiers and the Organisation Todt's own Protection Command. All tools and other equipment used by the workers were signed out and checked back in, normally by a member of the RSD. Access to the building site was by specially issued passes. To enable the work to continue around the clock, floodlights were brought into the site. To help keep the true nature of the work in which they were involved secret, workers' brigades were sent home or transferred to other construction sites after several months.

Ironically, it was at the *Wolfsschanze* that Todt died, being killed in February 1942 when his Heinkel He 111 crashed on take-off from Rastenburg airfield. Sabotage was suspected, though never proved, but from that date

Dr Todt speaking with a worker on a construction site on the Eastern Front.

onwards before any flight Hitler's fleet of aircraft was searched for suspicious packages.

The Rastenburg airport is some 4km from Rastenburg and from the *Wolfsschanze*. The airport was originally built for sports aviation in 1935 and was not suitable for Hitler's personal aircraft (the *Führermachine*) a large, four-engine Focke-Wulf Fw 200C-4/U1 Condor. During the construction of the *Wolfsschanze*, the airport's concrete runways were extended and strengthened but until this work was completed, Gerdauen airfield some 20 miles away was used, with Junkers Ju 52s providing a shuttle service with Rastenburg. The X format of the runways is still visible to this day. More than 200 buildings were built in the area around the airfield, which included, barracks, a power station, a radio station, a radar installation, a materials store with replacement engines, workshops and crew lounges. However, there were no runway lights at the airfield, which meant that landings could only take place during daylight. The senior officers of Hitler's air squadron, the *Fliegerstaffel des Führers*, such as SS-Gruppenführer Hans Baur, Hitler's personal pilot, as well as some of the crews, were quartered in private houses in the town.

According to Hans Baur, the Luftwaffe had up to twenty aircraft on the ground at Rastenburg, always ready for the use of Hitler and senior officers. Included among these were two other Condors to transport Hitler's staff when the Führer was on the move.[3] Also stationed at Rastenburg was the courier squadron (*kurierstaffel*) for the daily courier service from Berlin. This unit, commanded by Hauptmann Talk, was composed of between six and twelve fighter aircraft, which were also used for the rapid transport of messages and dispatches.

At the same time that work was undertaken on *Anlage Nord*, construction began at two other sites in Poland – *Anlage Mitte* (Camp Centre) and *Anlage Süd* (Camp South). *Anlage Mitte*, near the village of Konewka, north-east of the town of Tomaszów Mazowiecki, and *Süd* at Stępina, near Krosno, were only temporary sites for the protected parking of the *Führersonderzug* and Wehrmacht staff trains. Both of these sites had two similar complexes, a few kilometres from each other, built by Organisation Todt.

The complexes at *Anlage Süd* consisted of two long concrete bunkers built near the rail line between Rzeszów and Jasło for parking, and hiding, Hitler's train and *Atlas*, the train of the Armed Forces Operations Staff (*Wehrmachtführungsstabes*). The first of these massive facilities was a bunker located in the village of Stępina and the other was a tunnel cut through a hill by the town of Strzyżów. These two tunnels alone involved the employment of some 7,000 workers for almost a year, totalling 1.2 million days' labour.

The complex at *Anlage Mitte*, consisted of two bunkers at Konewka and Jelen. At Konewka were two pump houses, a news centre, a conference bunker, and several residential and service buildings.

Hitler's Condor at Immola Airfield, where he flew from Rastenburg to visit Marshal of Finland Baron Carl Gustaf Emil Mannerheim on his 75th birthday on 4 June 1942.

The tunnel/bunkers at all sites had a platform so that passengers could embark and disembark with ease. Each tunnel was in the region of 480m long, 8.3m wide and 12m high, with concrete walls 2m thick. The tunnel portals were protected by two-wing armoured doors with firing embrasures for the guards. With each site were a few huts and a complex of bunkers for power generation and water supply. Each site was surrounded by fences and wooden watchtowers and anti-aircraft gun positions, with other buildings used for personnel engaged in operations, administration, and maintenance.[4] The only times these sites were used by Hitler were on 27–28 August 1941, when *Amerika* was parked in the Strzyżów tunnel of *Anlage Süd*, while Mussolini's train was parked in the nearby bunker at Stępina, and a second time in October of that year. Other senior figures of the Third Reich, including Generalfeldmarschall Rommel and SS commander Heinrich Himmler, also used the tunnels.[5]

All the bunkers and the tunnel still survive and can be visited. The Konewka Bunker now houses a small collection of artefacts and of *Anlage Süd*, the one at Stępina is open to the public.[6]

One of the main reasons why the Görlitz forest had been chosen by Fritz Todt was the cover the woodland would provide, for security was of the greatest concern and dictated the entire nature of the complex. The forest, however, was only 2,000m wide and was not uniformly dense, and there were numerous open spaces, plus some trees had to be felled to create the space for

Hitler seen here greeting Mussolini at *Anlage Süd* on 27 August 1941.

'The artificial tunnel at Stępina.

A side tunnel branching off the main one at Stępina used as staff quarters.

Inside the Stępina tunnel. The tracks at both *Anlage Süd* and *Anlage Mitte* were covered over with wood after the war.

Another view of the tunnel at Stępina.

The entrance to the Konewka Bunker.

The Konewka bunker has been converted into a museum. The complex includes shelters for a generator, a boiler room, a water-pumping room, a well, a water cooler and a fuel tank.

Inside *Anlage Mitte*. The facilities were used in 1944 under the aliases 'Goldamsel' and 'Huhn' as ammunition storage and workshops for aircraft engines.

The camouflage that covered the tunnels helped conceal them from the air.

the installations. This meant that camouflage netting had to be hung from trees to the edges of the buildings to conceal the installations. Where there were insufficient trees to hang the netting, artificial ones were planted. The buildings themselves, of which there were eventually more than eighty in total, were also camouflaged. The complex covered approximately 2.5 square miles, only 4 per cent of which held buildings and other installations.

Most buildings constructed there had flat roofs with side walls 10–30cm high filled with soil. A specialist gardening company from Stuttgart, called Seidenspinner, was then employed to plant shrubs and lay grass, and even place more artificial trees, on the top of buildings, to give the impression from the air of an unbroken leafy canopy.[7] The roads and paths throughout the site, which were 2–3m wide, were also hidden with green camouflage nets, which were hung on eyelets that had been built into the sides of the buildings, and at night lighting along the roads was with navy blue electric lights on 2.5m-high concrete posts shaded from above. Rubbish baskets were placed at intervals along the paths. To aid orientation, most of the buildings were numbered, with those numbers being displayed on signposts. Those numbers are not the same as those seen on the buildings today.

The roads through the complex were based on the existing network of paths in the forest and, in principle, the buildings were not placed in parallel nor at right angles to each other to try and maintain the natural appearance of the forest from the air.

Although this photo was taken in July 1944 after the failed assassination attempt, the wall at the rear of the group shows what the camouflage was like at the time.

The camouflage, which was a mixture of seagrass, green dye and concrete, was so resilient that it can still be seen on many of the buildings.

A further example of the camouflage that covered the buildings can be seen here, as can the shutters that protected the windows. The man shaking hands with Hitler is Grand Admiral Karl Dönitz, who became Commander-in-Chief of the Navy (Oberbefehlshaber der Kriegsmarine) on 30 January 1943.

The tops of the lights in the *Wolfsschanze* were covered to conceal them from the air, one of which can be seen in the background of this photograph, which is of Marshal of Finland Carl Mannerheim in discussion with Hitler and Keitel, in the company of other German officers, during a visit to the *Wolfsschanze* in late June or early July 1942.

This evidently proved adequate, as the Wolf's Lair was never subjected to a serious attack from the air, and, despite Hitler's conviction that the Soviets knew about the site, the Red Army was seemingly unaware of the complex until they overran the site in early 1945.[8] Indeed, aerial photographs were taken to verify the effectiveness of the camouflage efforts, and chief of the OKW Generalfeldmarschall Wilhelm Keitel declared in his memoirs that: 'I have often flown over the site at various altitudes, but despite my precise knowledge of its location was never able to pin-point it from the air, except perhaps by the virtue of the lane leading through the forest and a single-track railway spur which had been closed to public traffic.'[9]

This did not stop Hitler becoming increasingly convinced that his enemies knew exactly where his headquarters were located: 'Hitler spoke more and more often of the possibility of a massive air raid on Führer headquarters,' wrote Traudl June in her memoirs. 'They know exactly where we are, and some time they're going to destroy everything here with carefully aimed bombs. I expect them to attack any day.'[10]

The Western Allies, through their intelligence and communications interception services, certainly did know the geographical location of the various *Führerhauptquartiere* and, should the USAAF or the RAF so have chosen, could have bombed the *Wolfsschanze*. But the distance from the air force bases in the UK was so great that only the heaviest bombers could have reached East Prussia, and they would have been without fighter escort. Raids on other targets in the east of Germany had resulted in very heavy losses among aircrew and any attempt to bomb the *Wolfsschanze* would have encountered stiff resistance. The question of dropping a 'blockbuster' bomb on the *Wolfsschanze* was certainly debated amongst the Allies but, as there was no guarantee that any such attack would have coincided with Hitler being in residence, the value of such an operation was highly questionable in light of the known risks, and the decision to bomb the *Wolfsschanze* was never taken.[11]

To further disguise the site's true purpose, all the people working in the construction of Wolf's Lair had civilian passports, and up until 21 June 1941, the day before the start of the invasion of the Soviet Union, civilian flights between Berlin and Moscow were permitted to fly over the site, including the scheduled operations of the Soviet airline Aeroflot. This added to the impression that the buildings in the forest had no real military significance, confirming them merely to being part of a chemical works.[12]

The road Keitel referred to ran from Rastenburg to Angerburg (today's Kętrzyn and Węgorzewo respectively), while the single-track railway was just to the north of the road and it too ran from Rastenburg to the small town of Görlitz. It was along these two avenues of communication that the material was transported that saw thousands of square metres of concrete poured, miles of cables installed, and tons of bricks laid across the vast site.

Initially, the buildings at the *Wolfsschanze* were of wood or concrete-and-brick structures with high windows protected by steel shutters. The ten main bunkers had concrete walls and roofs a metre thick that could withstand the impact of 500kg bombs. Heavy steel doors were made gas-tight with rubber seals, and there was overpressure in the bunkers to prevent the ingress of poisonous gas. There were also gas locks, and machine guns and pistol loops for defence. The floor in the rear of each of these bunkers was 2m below ground level and was used for sleeping, and at ground level was a small work room large enough for two desks.

As the site was developed, the wooden hutments were covered with brick walls and concrete roofs. Then, in 1944, many of the existing buildings were massively reinforced with concrete and steel shells at least 4m thick, inside which was a 2m-thick shock-absorbing sand or basalt insulation. A few additional bunkers were also built with the same level of protection. The ruins of these windowless bunkers are what visitors today can see today.

The *Wolfsschanze* had two central heating systems, and a pumping station on Lake Moysee provided the complex's water supply. The main bunkers, such as those of Hitler, Bormann, Keitel and so on, had their own emergency heating systems.

The site was constructed with three security zones. The outermost of these was Security Zone III (*Sperrkreis* III). This outer perimeter was surrounded by land and fencing and defended by the *Führer-Begleit-Bataillon* (FBB) with a strength in 1941 of 1,277, who manned slit trenches, guard houses, watch-towers and checkpoints. Beyond the perimeter of the complex was an extensive number of concrete gun emplacements strategically placed at road junctions and covering access roads. Armoured vehicles as well as troops on foot also made regular daily inspection trips along these roads.[13] The military formation responsible for guarding this area beyond *Sperrkreis* III was a battle-group (or *kampfgruppe*) under the command of Generalmajor Walter Denkert. In April 1943, a second unit was created to provide added security. This was the *Führergrenadierbataillon* (FGB).

The lakes and swampy ground that surround the forest might well have been excellent defensive features but, as we shall see, this also caused problems for the men and women living at the *Wolfsschanze* in the form of the ferocious mosquitos. On 14 June 1941, before Hitler and the permanent staff moved into the *Wolfsschanze*, an expert on dealing with mosquitos was

Work under way on the reinforcing of the bunkers.

flown in. What he did or recommended is not known, but he clearly failed to eradicate the problem.

Security Zone II (*Sperrkreis* II) was the area inside the outer security zone, with its buildings situated to the south of the railway line. There could be found the buildings of the *Wehrmachtführugsstab*, the Armed Forces Joint Staff, and the headquarters of the Commandant of the Wolf's Lair, Oberstleutnant Gustav Streve, and his staff. This was a self-contained area with its own dining and accommodation blocks. *Sperrkreis* II was surrounded by fencing but was not subject to any additional security controls. Commanded by General der Artillerie Walter Warlimont, deputy chief of the *Oberkommando der Wehrmacht*, the main function of the personnel in this area was to deliver pre-processed daily news and reports from all the theatres of war. These were then analysed by Hitler at his daily situation briefings.

Security Zone I (*Sperrkreis* I) was the most secure area of the Wolf's Lair. It was ringed by steel fencing and guarded by the RSD, which had overall responsibility for Hitler's security, and the SS-*Begleitkommando des Führers*, Hitler's personal bodyguard. Within it were eleven buildings, including the *Führerbunker* and bunkers for Hitler's closest associates, such as his secretary Martin Bormann, Chief of Operation Staff of the OKW Alfred Jodl, Reichsmarschall Göring and Keitel. Hitler's own accommodation was on the northern side of *Führerbunker* to shield the Führer from the direct sunlight he so detested. Both Hitler's and Keitel's bunkers had additional rooms where military conferences could be held.

There were other buildings scattered across the *Wolfsschanze* that were not within the fenced areas of *Sperrkreis* I or II. Generally speaking, most of the *Wolfsschanze* buildings had more than one entrance.

On 20 September 1943, security at the Wolf's Lair was tightened with the creation of an inner zone within *Sperrkreis* I, called *Sperrkreis* A or IA, by General der Infanterie Rudolf Schmundt, Hitler's adjutant and chief of the German Army Personnel Office. The only buildings in this new restricted zone apart from the *Führerbunker* were those of Generalfeldmarschall Keitel, the Führer's personal adjutants, Reichsleiter Martin Bormann, the security command centre, Dining Room I and the Tea House.

Before Hitler moved into the *Wolfsschanze*, 1. Bataillon Flak Regiment 604 arrived on 6 June 1941 to provide anti-aircraft protection.

The *Wolfsschanze* continued to be developed over the years of its occupation, with most of the brick buildings being covered in concrete in what is generally considered to be the second building phase in 1943. The third and final building stage the following year saw the main buildings turned into massive concrete structures, and when Hitler and his entourage returned there in the summer of 1944 because of the deteriorating situation on the Eastern Front, they were astonished at what they saw. 'The place was barely recognisable,' wrote Traudl Junge, one of Hitler's secretaries. 'Instead of the low-built little bunkers, heavy, colossal structures of concrete and iron rose above the trees, there was nothing to be seen from above. Grass had been planted on the flat rooftops, trees grew from the concrete, some of them real and some artificial, and from the plane you would have thought the forest stretched on unbroken.'[14] In total, the complex numbered more than eighty buildings, of which about forty were residential and commercial buildings, forty were light reinforced concrete storage bunkers and there were seven massive fortified structures.

Work on these improvements at the *Wolfsschanze* was still ongoing when Hitler visited his headquarters for the last time in the summer of 1944. Until his restructured bunker was ready for occupation, a new inner zone, the Führer Security Zone, was established in the north-west of *Sperrkreis* I, where Hitler resided temporarily in the bunker normally reserved for important guests.

As might be imagined, security was increased following the assassination attempt on 20 July 1944, and a detachment of the Liebstandarte-SS Adolf Hitler was assigned to the *Wolfsschanze* to support the FBB. The SS arrived with an array of weapons, including anti-tank guns, artillery, armoured vehicles, panzers, assault guns and tank destroyers.

Hitler himself gave his new *Führerhauptquartiere* its name as he travelled there for the first time. Hitler often liked to refer to himself as 'Herr Wolf', as Adolf in Old High German meant 'noble wolf', and three other headquarters included this reference to Hitler in their titles – the Werwolf at Vinnytsia in Ukraine, *Wolfsschlucht* I near Couvin, Belgium, and the *Wolfsschlucht* II near Soissons in France. *Schanze* means an entrenchment or fieldwork. So, more accurately, the *Wolfsschanze* (which is also spelt *Wolfschanze* on period documents and at the site itself) should be referred to as the Wolf's Field Fortification. These spellings contradict the spelling *Wolfsschlucht*, which is also used. It was in this massive field fortification that Hitler spent more than 800 days directing his war against the Soviet Union.

The prolonged effort against the Soviet Union was on such a massive scale that all the other key branches of the German military and intelligence services erected headquarters of their own in East Prussia within a 50km range of the *Wolfsschanze*. These included, as already mentioned, the headquarters of the Army at *Mauerwald*, as well as that of the Luftwaffe near Goldap, Himmler's SS near today's Pozezdrze, the German military intelligence service, Fremde Heere Ost, at Fortress Boyen, and that of the Chief of the Reich Chancellery, Hans Lammers, near the village of Radzieje, all of which will be examined in greater detail.

Chapter 2

Inside The Lair of the Wolf

Visitors to the *Wolfsschanze* usually arrived by train at the former Görlitz Bahnhof, which in earlier times had seen holidaymakers disembarking there for a small spa resort that became incorporated into the *Führerhauptquartiere* as the site took shape in late 1940 and early 1941. The station was situated to the south of the track and close to the western edge of the forest. The existing station platform was extended to take the *Führersonderzug* and two extra rail sidings were added, one of which was to accommodate the train when Hitler was in residence. The sidings were approximately 500m long. Among the improvements to the station was the addition of a signal box and several flak battery positions placed to the north of the station.

During the period which the *Wolfsschanze* was in use, every night two identical courier trains (*Führer-Kurierzug*) left from Silesia Station in Berlin and the town of Angerburg in East Prussia. The trains passed through Görlitz, arriving at the opposite destination the following morning.

At Görlitz, one locomotive was kept with steam up whenever Hitler was in residence and the complete train could be coupled up and on the move in under two hours. When Hitler's train was in the siding it was, of course, covered in camouflage netting to disguise it from the air. As the war progressed, the line was also used for military evacuation and replenishment trains.

Hitler arrived at the *Wolfsschanze* for the first time on *Führersonderzug Amerika* in the early hours of 24 June 1941. It was at 01.30 hours that the Führer and elements of his staff first set foot inside the *Wolfsschanze*, having been driven by a fleet of vehicles the short distance from the station, little more than a day after the start of Operation *Barbarossa*.

It was just a short walk, or drive, from the station along the Rastenburg to Angerburg road to the Officers' Guard Post, the *Offizierwache*. Here there was sign that read: 'The persons which enter this area must report at the Commandant's Guard Post'. At that point there was a pole-barrier across the road and only when the officer on duty was satisfied that visitors had due cause to be admitted into the *Wolfsschanze* was the pole raised, allowing the visitors to continue to the western entrance, the *Wache West*, after crossing over the railway line. Just to the south of the Officers' Guard Post was a barracks for the RSD. Led by Gruppenführer Johann Rattenhuber under the overall command of Himmler, the RSD's role was that of providing personal

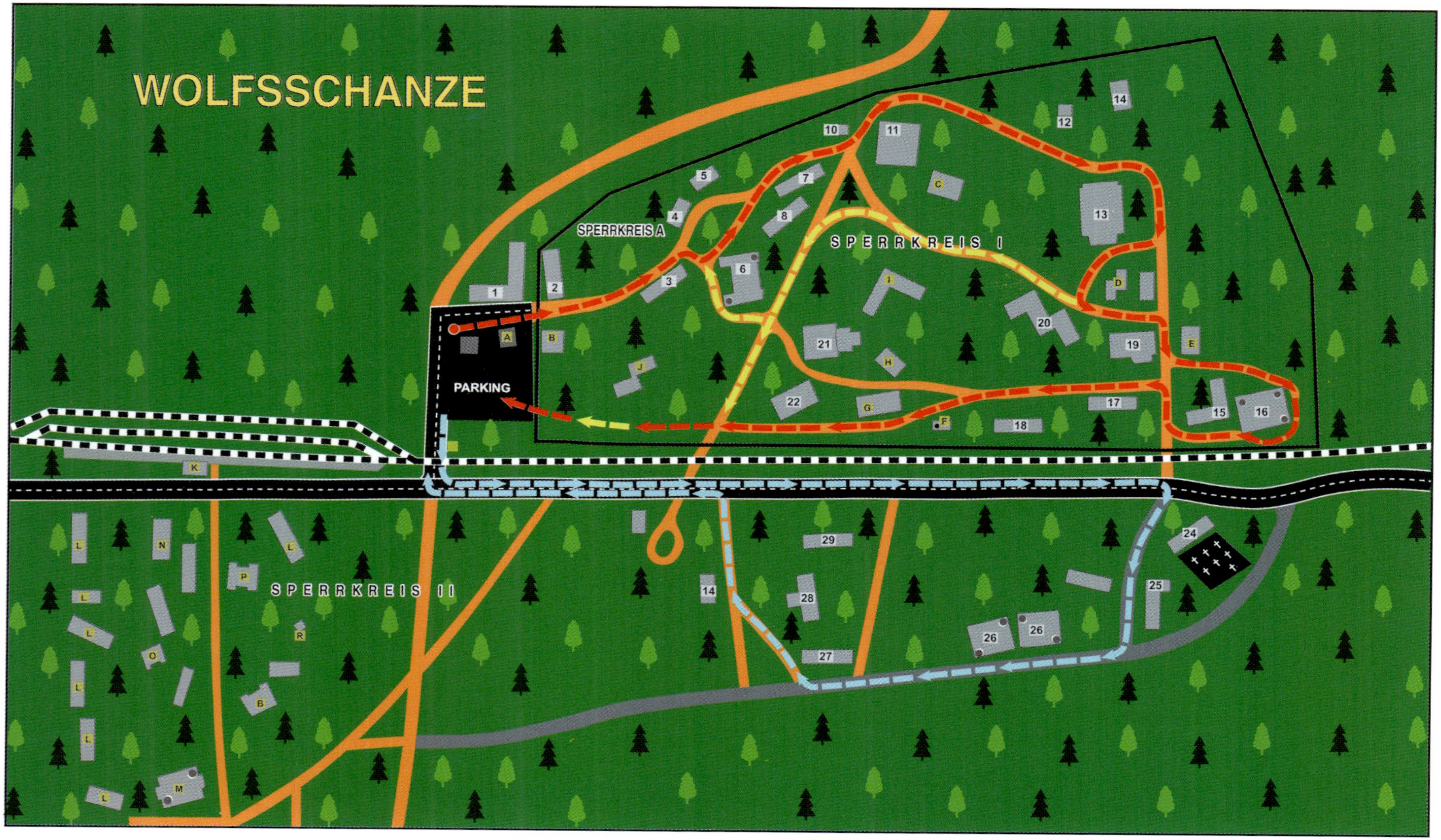
WOLFSSCHANZE
SPERRKREIS A
SPERRKREIS I
SPERRKREIS II
PARKING

Members of Hitler's bodyguard wait at the *bahnhof* for the arrival of a train, in this instance the approaching train is carrying the Italian leader Benito Mussolini.

Benito Mussolini, Hitler and Hermann Göring on the platform of the *bahnhof* at the *Wolfsschanze* on 30 August 1941. Walking behind them is Generalfeldmarschall Keitel.

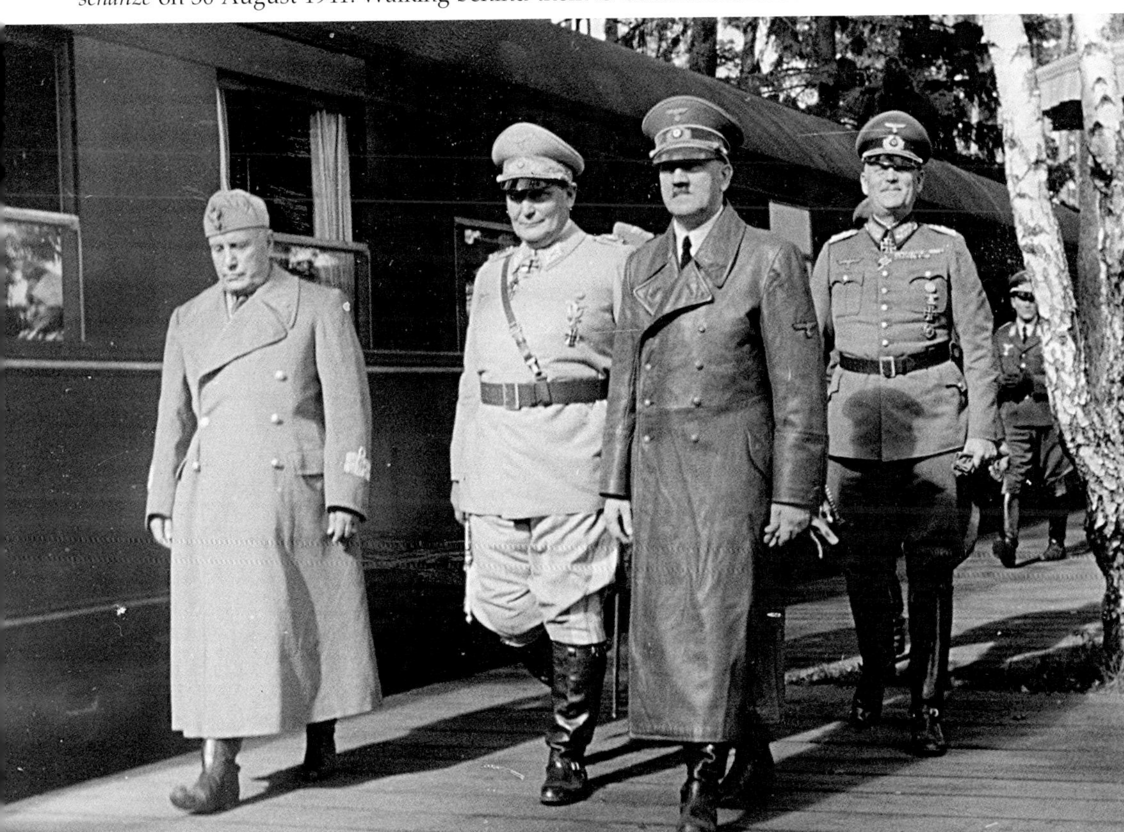

Visitors came from far afield to the *Wolfsschanze* and mostly arrived by train. Here, the Croatian Minister of Foreign Affairs, Stijepo Perić, is greeted at the *bahnhof* at the start of an official visit to meet Hitler in March 1944. Perić was accompanying the Croatian Prime Minister, Momčilo Mandić.

The King of Bulgaria, Boris III, is greeted at the *Wolfsschanze bahnhof* during an official visit to Hitler, 26 March 1942.

The ruins of the *bahnhof* buildings and platform, the track is just visible in the distance.

The plaster still holds on some of the walls of the *bahnhof*.

The *bahnhof* is not on the designated visitor trails and is slowly being consumed by nature. Its position on the map is marked as **Building K**.

The station platform as viewed from the track.

Hitler crossing the track in conversation with Albert Speer on his right-hand side, on 18 May 1942.

When in use by Hitler, the daily courier service that passed through the *bahnhof* was listed on the German railway timetables. The original track was destroyed in 1945 but after the war the Polish authorities replaced the single track and for a period ran a service to Angerburg, which is what can be seen today.

Two photographs showing deep cellars at the station. These structures were rare due to the swampy nature of the ground.

Inside the main station building.

This photograph was taken on 27 June 1942, quite possibly by the *Wache West* entrance. The visitor being greeted by Hitler is Gustav Mannerheim, commander-in-chief of Finland's armed forces. He would have been driven from the station in the Mercedes (painted in dull olive grey) in the background.

protection for Hitler and other leading Nazis. Rattenhuber was also responsible for securing all Hitler's field headquarters.

Following behind Hitler's party on the morning of 24 June 1941 with another of the various echelons of staff officers was Generalmajor Walter Warlimont, who arrived by train at 03.45 hours: 'The detraining point was a halt on a local line and only a few hundred yards away we found the new HQ Area 2 [*Sperrkreis* II]. It was entirely surrounded by high barbed-wire fencing and was hardly visible from the road.'[1]

There were just three entrances to the *Wolfsschanze*, the southern (*Wache Süd*) and eastern (*Wache Ost*) being the others. Visitors arriving by air would fly into Rastenburg airfield from where they would be driven initially through *Wache Süd* and then *Wache West*. It was through *Wache Ost* that personnel left for or arrived from OKH *Mauerwald*, SS *Hochwald*, and Göring's *Hauptquartier, Robinson*, usually by train, the railway line having been extended and diverted to link together all the headquarters sites in the region, on which railcars were operated.

Having passed through the checkpoints, vehicles would drive into a small compound where there was a garage for the vehicles (**Building No. 22**) and an accommodation block for drivers, pilots and mechanics (**Building G**). Additional covered car parking spaces were distributed across the entire site in case of air raids.

At this early stage of the war on the Eastern Front, the *Wolfsschanze* was far from complete, as Walter Warlimont explained: 'The majority of the officers were in wooden huts around a simple country inn, in normal times a visiting spot for the people of Rastenburg ... the regulations governing the Berlin Ministries had been followed as regards size of rooms, numbers of windows and furnishings. Even more remarkable was a semi-underground construction looking like a long railway sleeping car with a row of doors side by side; this proved to contain additional offices and sleeping accommodation for the officers.'

As a senior officer, Warlimont had a double room. He described how inside the rooms the concrete walls were covered with wooden panelling painted in 'cheerful' colours, and that there were baths and wash basins with running water, built-in cupboards, heating and every type of electrical gadget. As he remarked, it was hardly the normal picture of a Spartan field headquarters.

Warlimont, however, did not like the confines of the *Wolfsschanze*, which he called 'this catacomb', and after just a few nights he went to stay in the *Führersonderzug*, and later to the former spa hotel (what he referred to as the country inn) where, surprisingly, the old proprietor still lived. Before long, the other members of Warlimont's Section L joined him, and together they formed their own little officers' mess.

A driver from OKH *Mauerwald* described his journey to the *Wolfsschanze*: 'The way led via Rastenburg, from there towards Lötzen. After about 3km,

Building No. 22, the garage or *garagen*.

The garage could accommodate up to sixteen cars.

An intriguing photograph of Nazi Gauleiters at the *Wolfsschanze* on 7 February 1943. It is possible Hitler greeted the arrivals in the vehicle compound.

through small villages, I approached a dark, mixed forest. After a few hundred metres, a large barrier blocked the road. It was *Wache West*, which was the post through which everything entered and left the *Wolfsschanze* … A guard stood at the barrier, to whom I showed my ID and my orders … After a short telephone call, he returned both and I was able to pass.'[2]

Today, visitors (which, in pre-pandemic times numbered more than 200,000 each year) are directed to a car and coach park that is situated at what was the entrance to *Sperrkreis* I, where a security barrier, known as *Tor* I, guarded the roadway into this most secure of areas. There was only one other entrance to *Sperrkreis* I, which was at the opposite, or eastern side, of the security zone, and was known as *Tor* II.

A large map of the complex in the car park indicates three routes that visitors can take. The red-marked route is the one most commonly used by tourists. It runs for a distance of around 1.8km, past all major buildings that were in the former *Sperrkreis* I. This tour takes about seventy minutes.

The yellow/red route is shorter, at 1.3km, and is intended for visitors who principally only want to see Hitler's bunker and where the 20 July 1944 assassination attempt took place. This route can be walked in fifty minutes or less.

The blue/red marked route takes in most of *Sperrkreis* I and *Sperrkreis* II past the majority of the buildings in the *Wolfsschanze* and covers a distance of 2.4km. Visitors should allow two and half hours for this walk.

It is also possible to detour off the beaten path to investigate other parts of the *Wolfsschanze*, though this would only be practicable for the able-bodied and it must be pointed out that this is potentially dangerous and that each individual that leaves the marked routes does so entirely at their own risk, as they do in entering any of the ruins in the unmarked areas.

Here also can still be seen the quarters, or barracks, of the Führer Escort Battalion, the *Führer-Begleit-Bataillon*, or FBB (**Building No. 1**). The FBB protected Hitler's military headquarters and accompanied him when visiting battlefronts. The building accommodated fifty men. In general, the FBB defended the outer perimeter, *Sperrkreis* III. The FBB was increased to brigade strength (becoming the *Führerbegleitbrigade*) in November 1944. In the event of the alarm being sounded on the warning of any perceived threat, all the men were to make their way immediately to Hitler's bunker.

The ruins of Hitler's personal air-raid shelter can be seen in the north-eastern corner of the car park (**Building No. 0**). Until the development of the massive reinforced bunkers in 1944, the early buildings were not safe against heavy aerial bombardment, which explains why Hitler needed an air-raid shelter.

It is not possible to enter Building No. 0.

Also in the grounds of the car park is a bunker that held an emergency power generator (*notstromzentrale*) **Building A**.

Building No. 1 was only erected in 1944. It is now a hotel and restaurant.

Opposite No. 1 is the barracks of the *Führerbegleitkommando*, or FKB (**Building No. 2**). The FKB along with the RSD were responsible for security within *Sperrkreises* I and the personal safety of the Führer. Wherever Hitler went these men were always in close proximity. They had to keep just far enough away so that they could not hear his conversations with the people accompanying him, but close enough to be able to intervene immediately if the Führer was in danger. Men of the FKB were the only persons allowed to carry arms in Hitler's presence.

Across from these barracks on the other side of the path is **Building B**, which was a bunker that held an emergency electricity generator, now a souvenir and gift shop. This point marks the start of the red route and also the beginning of Sperrkreis I.

Only official vehicles were permitted into *Sperrkreis* I, and those belonging to senior Reich leaders and, in terms of the military, only field marshals and above. All others, including generals in their staff cars, had to disembark and then be escorted on foot to the entrance, where their credentials were checked. High-ranking German officers who had a meeting with Hitler but did not have quarters at the *Wolfsschanze* were often accommodated at the Hunters' Lodge hotel near the town of Angerburg on the shore of Lake Schwenzeitsee

Building No. 2

Some indication of how Hitler's bodyguard maintained close watch over the Führer can be seen as Otto Günsche, Hitler's valet who was a member of the *Führerbegleitkommando*, walks just a few feet behind Hitler but discreetly keeping his distance.

(today's Święcajty), which is one of the Masurian lakes adjoining Lake Mamry. This was described by Alexander Stahlberg as 'a beautiful, gracious wooden house' which had served as a residence for Field Marshal von Brauchitsch, the Commander-in-Chief of the Army, until his dismissal in December 1941.

The *Wolfsschanze* was still being developed when Hitler moved in and workmen were unavoidably present even in *Sperrkreis* I despite the stringent security measures in place. The workers, of course, had to be able to walk around but were not allowed to get too close to the bunkers. Only Hitler's and Keitel's bunkers had a permanent guard posted at their respective entrances. If an urgent maintenance or repair was necessary, which meant workers having to enter one of the bunkers, they were accompanied at all times by a member of the FKB or the RSD.

The wire perimeter of all three *Sperrkreis* was patrolled day and night. In *Sperrkreis* I the FBK and the RSD mounted a round-the-clock surveillance, and stood guard over whichever building Hitler was in. These troops also acted as orderlies for those living and working in *Sperrkreis* I. When guarding Hitler, the men of the FBK were on duty for twenty-four hours, rotating two or three hours on and two or three hours off during that time. The normal shift started and ended at 17.00 hours. The following day was a rest day. A full platoon was on duty at any one time. It was standard practice to place each sentry within visible distance of the next sentry.

Those entitled to enter the facility who did not permanently reside or work there had to be thoroughly vetted before being granted passes. There were two types of passes – a permanent pass and a temporary pass, the latter being for either a day, week or month. Intriguingly, Göring and Foreign Minister Ribbentrop, both of whom spent little time at the Wolf's Lair, were granted only day passes.

As mentioned earlier, any visitors to *Sperrkreis* I were escorted to the building they were attending by members of the FKB or RSD that stood by to perform this duty as required. According to Hauptmann Guam of the 3rd Panzer Grenadier Battalion of the FBB, the guards were frequently tested for their alertness by bogus officers.[3]

Despite the severity of the security measures, there were a number of unfortunate lapses. One such was on 9 July 1943, when a Polish peasant called Jozef Frazewski was shot dead by the guards. He somehow managed to get into the *Wolfsschanze* without reporting at any checkpoint and was seen only as he was heading directly for *Sperrkreis* I, when he was then gunned down, being hit in the head and thigh, dying instantly. Frazewski was carrying a haversack when he was shot but, according to the report of the Geheimen Feldpolizei, all that was inside the haversack were several pounds of bread and some cold meat. In his pockets were 93 Reich Marks, an old knife, a matchstick and some tobacco. What Frazewski's intentions were remains a mystery.[4]

In the same year another security breach occurred with a colonel of the army. He was on his way by train to OKH *Mauerwald* and, never having travelled to the area before, got out of the train when it stopped at the *Wolfsschanze*. Unfazed by his unfamiliar surroundings, he wandered into the dining room in Sperrkreis I, where he was innocently enjoying breakfast with Hitler's naval adjutant, Konteradmiral Karl Jesco von Puttkammer, when he saw Hitler walking by. Only then was it realised that the colonel was somewhere he was not supposed to be.

On one evening in August 1943, a Polish woman walked along the railway track past the guard at the east entrance just as the changeover of the guard between shifts was taking place. She walked all the way along the track through the *Wolfsschanze* and it was only when she reached the *Wache West* entrance that she was stopped and arrested.[5]

There was also the remarkable story of the Polish woman Jaroslawa Mirowska. Following the invasion of Poland, Mirowska became friendly with SS-Gruppenführer Hermann Fegelein who, in turn, was close to Himmler and later married Eva Braun's sister Gretl. Though considered one of the Third Reich's most prominent women, she was in fact working as an agent for the

Polish Underground resistance under the codename *Erika II*. She also became acquainted with SS-Gruppenführer Wilhelm Bittrich, who invited her to join him on a trip to East Prussia in July 1942. Bittrich visited the *Wolfsschanze*, taking Mirowska with him.

In a camp composed predominantly of men, the attractive woman was not just invited to eat with the officers, but she was escorted all over the site. Carefully observing the layout of the *Wolfsschanze*, upon her return to Warsaw, Mirowska was able to compile an accurate a report on Hitler's headquarters. It is said that this was forwarded to London, but the British did not share this information with any of their allies.[6]

As mentioned earlier, on 20 September 1943, a special Führer Restricted Area, *Sperrkreis* A, or IA, was created within *Sperrkreis* I, within which were just seven buildings.

The only people that could enter *Sperrkreis* A on a regular basis were persons that served Hitler directly and those who had their offices there, and these individuals were issued with special passes. Likewise, the list of permanent lunch guests in Dining Room I was limited to the Führer's immediate suite.

Additional passes could be issued by the HQ Commandant but only with permission of Rudolph Schmundt, or his deputy, and in consultation with SS-Obergruppenführer Julius Schaub or his deputy. There were three gates leading into *Sperrkreis* A, at Keitel's, the adjutants' and Bormann's buildings, and were each manned by one non-commissioned officer of the FBB and one RSD officer. It was their responsibility to check all passes. Passes were of different shapes and colours and print, and the designs were changed frequently.

In addition, an RSD official was constantly patrolling *Sperrkreis* A, who was responsible for ensuring that no one was there without authorisation. Anyone found without a pass would be arrested and interrogated.

The only vehicles allowed in *Sperrkreis* A, other than those of the persons that lived and worked there, were those belonging to senior Reich officials and officers of the rank of field marshal (generalfeldmarschall). These individuals and their drivers and other accompanying persons all had to have valid passes. The only other vehicles permitted to enter *Sperrkreis* A were lorries bringing in supplies and, of course, these were carefully vetted, and all drivers and assistants were required to obtain passes.

In an emergency, it was possible for an individual to enter without a pass, but in such circumstances one of the RSD officers had to take the visitor where he was going and bring him back afterwards.

Guests for luncheons or meals in the Dining Room or Teahouse could come only if asked by Schuab or Schmundt after permission or a request from the Führer, and applications had to be made well in advance. Persons ordered to come to the Führer or to an agency in *Sperrkreis* A had to wait in Dining Room II in *Sperrkreis* II and were treated as guests of the Führer.

There were no guards of any description actually inside any of the buildings of *Sperrkreis* I or *Sperrkreis* A, only outside. Though before the assassination attempt of 20 July there were no body or bag searches, it was merely customary upon entering a building for visitors to remove their cap and holster along with the associated side arms.

To man this additional zone, it seems that more guards were needed and a platoon from one of the Army's infantry divisions was added to the FBB, apparently without any prior security vetting. One of those men was 21-year-old Kurt Salterberg. Surprising as it seems, he and some of his comrades manned the entry gate into *Sperrkreis* A, the most important of all the zones. They operated around the clock as per the other guards. Salterberg's shift ran: 11.00–14.00; 17.00–20.00; 23.00–02.00; 05.00–08.00. According to Salterberg, two men stood at the entry point while a third man toured *Sperrkreis* A, checking in with the men at the entrance every thirty minutes. The men were armed only with pistols.[7] Another member of the FBB, Wilhelma Gerke, states that men on duty were armed with a machine gun with six magazines and two hand grenades.[8]

After the 20 July assassination attempt, there were a number of organisational changes in the field of security regulations. This included the appointment of Major Otto Ernst Remer (who had been instrumental in obstructing the plotters in Berlin) to the position of 'Combat' Commandant. Promoted to colonel, and placed under his command, were the *Führer-Grenadier-Bataillon*, the *Führer-Flak-Abteilung*, the *Führer-Luftnachrichten-Abteilung* and other units. Remer was under the command of the Commandant of the *Wolfsschanze*, Colonel Gustav Streve, but was entirely responsible for the protection of the *Führerhauptquartiere*.

The next building along the road is probably the most notable of all the structures in the *Wolfsschanze* and possibly the most visited, for it was here that Oberst Claus von Stauffenberg placed a bomb that almost killed Hitler on 20 July 1944. A fuller description of the events leading up to and during that fateful day will be given later.

This building (**Building No. 3**) was a standard Wehrmacht rectangular, brick-built *lagebarache*, or barracks, 12.5m long by 14.5m wide and 5m high. In 1943 concrete was added to the walls and roof of this basic structure. The concrete was a metre thick on the roof and half a metre thick on the walls, with a cavity between the walls and the interior wooden panelling of about 6cm.[9] It became known as the situation conference room.

It held a large, 1.2m × 6m oak card table in the middle, the top of which was about 8–10cm thick and was held up by three supports, which were also about 8–10cm thick. These supports were made of one piece of wood, which effectively united two table legs; their height was 80–100cm and they went

The first ruins encountered are those of 'armoured transporter posts' on the right-hand side of the road.

almost through the whole width of the table, about 120–150cm.[10] The significance of these dimensions will be seen in due course.

The other furnishing in the room on 20 July 1944 included twenty chairs and stools with straw wicker seating. At the right front corner in the entrance, as viewed upon entry, was a round table approximately 110cm in diameter, a telephone, wastebaskets, lamps, on the left a music and radio cabinet, and a desk. The exact number of windows has, it would seem, not been determined. It has been estimated that the number would have been between five and nine, with one on the east side and between four and eight on the north-facing side. There are memorials to the assassination attempt next to the building's ruins.

This strengthening of building No. 3 took place during the second phase of the development of the *Wolfsschanze* when, in August 1943, the OT Oberbauleitung Rastenburg engaged various construction companies in the large-scale expansion and reinforcement of the bunker buildings, mainly to encase them in concrete shells. At the same time, the bunkers of other surrounding headquarters such as *Mauerwald* and *Hochwald* were also adapted to protect against the new, heavier, Allied bombs. Around 3,600 workers from more than 500 companies worked day and night in the Görlitz forest for months.

Building No. 3.

The roof of Building No. 3. From the outside the building appeared to be a concrete structure but in reality it was a standard Luftwaffe barrack made of wood and brick that was further protected with a concrete outer skin. The ceiling and inner walls of the barracks were clad with soft fibre panels.

As originally designed, the working bunkers were generally built with a narrow corridor leading from the entrances, of which there were two, to the workroom, inside which there was room for two desks. The dormitory bunkers, lined with wood panels, were each about the size of a railway sleeping car berth and were furnished with a bed, wash basin, fitted wardrobe and telephone. A tiled toilet/bathroom was situated near the entrance.[11]

The road branches here with a side path on the left leading to **Building No. 4**. This was the accommodation block of the RSD, close to which was the accommodation bunker of the officers of the FBK and Hitler's personal servants (**Building No. 5**).

Retracing one's steps takes the visitor back to the main red route and to **Building No. 6,** which was the guest bunker for visiting VIPs, the Gästebunker. This massive structure was heavily reinforced during the third remodelling period. A number of notable people stayed in the guest bunker. These included, as one might predict, Mussolini and his Foreign Minister, Ciano, and the leaders of other Axis countries such as Hungary's Miklós Kállay, and Prince Kyril of Bulgaria, but also some less expected individuals.

Another photograph taken during the visit of Gustav Mannerheim on 27 June 1942. As can be seen, some of the early buildings were far different from the flat-roofed buildings usually associated with those in *Sperrkreis* I and II and those seen today in the *Wolfsschanze*.

The simple nature of the early barracks can be seen in this photograph of Field Marshal von Brauchitsch (second from the left) and other senior German officers accompanying the Hungarian Regent, Miklós Horthy, on his visit to the *Wolfsschanze* on 8 September 1941.

Another view of the early barracks in the background of this photograph of Hermann Göring and Walther von Brauchitsch also taken in September 1941.

Building No. 4.

Building No. 5.

One such was Subhas Chandra Bose, who visited Hitler at the *Wolfsschanze* in May 1942. Bose was an India nationalist leader whose opposition to British rule led to him being placed under house arrest. In 1940, he escaped and made his way to Germany. With the help of the Germans, Bose set up the Free India Radio in Berlin, from where he delivered nightly broadcasts urging Indians to rise up and throw off the Imperial British yolk. There was, of course, no possibility of Germany ever invading India, however, the astonishing successes of Japanese forces in 1941–42 offered Bose hope that the British could be driven out of India and he wanted to return to Asia to join the Japanese. Bose travelled to the *Wolfsschanze* seeking a meeting with Hitler to gain the Führer's approval for his journey, which he obtained. He was taken by U-boat to Madagascar in February 1943, where he boarded a Japanese submarine, being taken to the Japanese-held island of Sumatra. He became Commander-in-Chief of the Indian National Army, which fought alongside the Japanese in Burma. He died in a plane crash at the end of the war.

One of the duties of the troopers of the FBK when acting as orderlies involved taking drinks to guests in the guest bunker. One of the troopers, called Eduard Krenz, was the proud owner of a bicycle and he set up a fast drinks service, balancing the drinks on a tray. This went very well until one

The Prime Minister of Hungary, Miklós Kállay, being welcomed to the *Wolfsschanze* by Hitler, circa 6 June 1942. As can be seen, the forest was far from universally dense.

The visit of Subhas Chandra Bose was recorded for posterity, the Indian nationalist leader shown shaking hands with Hitler in the Führer's study.

Building No. 6 is one of seven windowless heavy bunkers scattered across the *Wolfsschanze*. Its enormous dimensions of 45m × 27m with a foundation depth of about 5m and a roof strength of 5.5m bore no relation to the confined usable area in its interior. In the last phase of construction in 1944, shortly before the assassination attempt, the strengthening work on Hitler's bunker was not yet finished, so Hitler resided in the *Gästebunker* from 14 July until 8 November 1944.

Some indication of the enormous amount of concrete used on the *Gästebunker* in its final form can be gauged by the thickness of the damaged walls.

Here the steel reinforcing bars are exposed.

Such was the strength of the guest bunker in its final stages, the attempt at destroying it in January 1945 made little impression on parts of the massive walls.

It is only when stood in front of the guest bunker isit really possible to gauge its true scale.

One of the entrances to the guest bunker.

Inside the guest bunker.

So heavy was the roof that the supporting walls inside were correspondingly thick.

Part of the roof of the guest bunker, showing the supporting girders.

This appears to have been an annex attached to the bunker.

A metal ladder on the side of the guest bunker leads to the roof where two light anti-aircraft guns were mounted.

On the roof of the Guest Bunker.

day he almost collided with a group of officers. Krenz, the bike, the tray, and of course the drinks, all flew spectacularly through the air. Apparently, this kept everyone in *Sperrkreis* I chuckling for days.

Behind (to the north) the *Gästebunker* along the red route is **Building No. 8**, which served as both a post office and the quarters of the chief of the RSD, Rattenhuber.

Adjacent to No. 8 is the Stenographers' barracks – *Stenographenbarake* – **Building No. 7**. Stenographers were people who wrote and transcribed shorthand and typed it up, in this case the notes from the situation conferences regarding the fighting in the East.

In the autumn of 1942, there was a major disagreement between Hitler and Jodl concerning Army Group A when he was at his 'Werwolf' headquarters at Vinnytsia. He was convinced that this had been caused by a misinterpretation of his instructions by the stenographers. As a result, Hitler ordered that both the daily briefings and all other conversations concerning the conduct of the war should be recorded verbatim and typed up as such. He said that this would also enable people in the future to study his method of warfare. For this a dozen additional stenographers were brought in from the Reichstag and put to work in pairs, taking down every word that was said at the situation conferences.

That there had been a misunderstanding of Hitler's intentions was, according to Heinz Linge, quite understandable: 'When in Hitler's presence, it was of great importance to know or anticipate his needs. This could not always be inferred from his instructions and orders. "Thinking aloud" he would bring

As can be seen from these two photographs, Building No. 8 was a simple brick structure, like most of those in the *Wolfsschanze*.

The roof of No. 8, as with most of the buildings, was heavily reinforced with concrete.

The routes through the *Wolfsschanze* generally followed the existing forest tracks.

The *Stenographenbarake* was some 50m long by 14m wide.

Because of the highly sensitive nature of the material handled by the stenographers, there was added security in the form of a fence that surrounded the building. The entrance into the stenographers' compound was through a gate that was under guard and only authorised personnel were permitted access.

Though the buildings in the *Wolfsschanze* varied depending on their use, many were of a basically standard rectangular size. One of those standard barracks buildings can be seen in this photograph of Hitler with Generalfeldmarschall Fedor von Bock, which is believed to have been taken on 18 January 1942.

The *Stenographenbarake* was another brick structure with a very thick concrete roof.

to light individual problems from all directions and make simple procedures into the most insoluble problems. He presented each position in such a way that an uninitiated listener who was not familiar with his methods could often not know what he actually wanted. He would wander off the subject, talk about irrelevancies and confuse people who were following his explanations closely. Mostly, he left it to his listener to put the right "weight" on a thing and so understand what it was he had been talking about. Even the military, who are normally used to terse and clear commands, sometimes had to endure an hour or two of explanations and they would still be uncertain what he really wanted.'[12]

Though most of those who worked at the *Wolfsschanze* complained of the conditions, one stenographer was very impressed with its East Prussian setting: 'How beautiful it is out here,' wrote Karl Thöt. 'The whole site is resplendent with luscious greenery. The woods breathe a magnificent tranquillity. The wooden huts, including ours, have by now [1944] been heavily bricked-in to afford protection against bomb splinters. We all feel at ease here. It's become a second home to us.'[13]

Continuing northwards, on the left side of the road a staircase can be seen that leads to two below ground level and still well-preserved storage rooms. This is **Building No. 10**.

Building No. 10.

The food storage rooms, or *vorratsraum*, of Building 10 have a total area of 80 sq m.

Directly opposite No. 10 are the ruins of Martin Bormann's bunker (**Building No. 11**). Described by Traudel Junge as 'a thick-set, bull-necked man', Bormann, as Hitler's private secretary, controlled all access to Hitler and whose named appeared on all the instructions and orders relating to the organisation of the *Wolfsschanze*. To maintain his influence over Hitler, Bormann ensured that there was no permanent accommodation in *Sperrkreis* I for either Himmler or Göring, who, as we shall shortly see, had their own bunkers in the area outside *Sperrkreis* II.

Building No. 11.

One of the entrances to Bormann's bunker.

Two views of the main internal passage inside Bormann's bunker.

The exterior walls of Bormann's bunker. It was said that large bunkers such as Bormann's could withstand a direct hit from any known bomb of that era.

Bormann's bunker in its final stage in 1944, like other large ones, was built with an external shell and an inner core filled with basalt that was to absorb the shock from heavy explosions, thus protecting the central rooms. It is very noticeable that inside these massive structures the rooms are quite small in relation to the size of the buildings, and this is because of these thick multiple layers of protection. At the time these large bunkers were built, it was estimated that the only way that they could be destroyed would have been by a sustained aerial bombardment that would create large craters immediately next to the bunkers, so that the bunkers would tip in, destroy the underground communication cables, with the occupants being buried alive.[14] Lodged with Bormann in this building was his assistant and four secretaries. From his bunker, Bormann had telephone contact with every Gauleiter in Germany, as well as with the staff in the Nazi Party offices in Berlin and Munich.[15]

While Hitler had a relatively modest lifestyle, some of the higher-ranking Wehrmacht and SS officers led a dissolute and luxurious life. It was claimed, however, that Bormann's opulent lifestyle exceeded all others, not least in his house next to his bunker, the remains of which are shown below.

Close to Bormann's bunker are the ruins of his personal residence, **Building C**.

Bormann was known for his fine food and drink, and especially for his women, choosing particularly attractive girls as his 'secretaries' – most of whom were replaced fairly frequently. His wife, Gerda, knew of his affairs, philosophically conceding that: 'My husband needs it.'

It is no coincidence that the next building along the road from Bormann's bunker was Hitler's bunker (**Building No. 13**). Hitler's apartment consisted of a workroom or study, a meeting room, a bedroom, a few smaller rooms for servants, a corridor, a shower and toilet. In 1942 the *Führerbunker* received a wooden extension in which there was a conference room where, from November 1942, some briefings were held. His quarters were far from luxurious, as his valet, Hauptsturmführer Heinz Linge, well remembered: 'As everywhere, Hitler set himself up as the yardstick. If a stranger to FHQ *Wolfsschanze* did not know better and saw Hitler's bedroom with its military-issue field bed, he would have thought it to be the dormitory of a subaltern. After having had the opportunity to peer briefly behind the scenes and shaking his head in amazement, Generalfeldmarschall von Bock once said to me: 'Our infantry at the front should see this.'[16] The only other object in his bedroom was a crate for his dog, Blondi.

One ordinary soldier did, in fact, get an opportunity to see inside Hitler's bunker, and his account confirms that of Heinz Linge. This occurred in 1942

Hitler in discussion with Finnish General Harald Öhquist at the Wolf's Lair in 1941. From left to right: Wilhelm Keitel, Walther von Hewel, Ribbentrop's representative at the *Wolfsschanze*, Hitler, Öhquist, Joachim von Ribbentrop and Hitler's adjutant, Gerhard Engel.

when Hitler was at his 'Werwolf' headquarters in Ukraine. After a night shift, Alfons Schultz, who was a telephone operator in the Reich press centre, was walking past the *Führerbunker* when he saw it was being guarded only by an SS officer whom he knew well and he persuaded his friend to let him peep inside: 'Hitler's bedroom was spartan. I only saw a camo bed, a shelf with two books, a cupboard, a laundry corner, a table and two chairs. I was interested in the literature with which "*mein* Führer" was busy. Disappointed, I discovered that it was two works on stomach disease.'[17] This austerity did not impress Walter Warlimont, however, who described Hitler's room as 'gloomy'. This was possibly because all the windows in Hitler's bunker faced north to avoid direct sunlight. Hitler did eventually permit himself a small luxury in the form of a gramophone, on which Beethoven was often played as well as Strauss, Hugo Wold and, of course, Wagner.[18]

Before it was sealed in with its concrete shell in 1944, Otto Günsche, who became one of Hitler's valets in January 1943, described the *Führerbunker*: 'Around 105 metres square, it had several large windows on one side, and a long map table. Between the windows there were telephones on wires with additional headsets. Besides Hitler's desk, the room contained a round fireside table and two safes, one set in the wall, the other free standing. On the walls there were three large topographical maps.'[19]

One of those maps on the wall can be seen in this photograph taken on 15 September 1943. The man shaking hands with Hitler is Oberst Walther Lange, receiving the Knight's Cross of the Iron Cross with Oak Leaves from the Führer.

A wonderful view of what is possibly Hitler's 'gramophone'. It appears, in fact to be a radiogram. In this photograph Großadmiral Erich Johann Albert Raeder is in discussion with Hitler in February 1943.

Gunsche also described Hitler's bunker after its 1944 redevelopment: 'There was a real maze inside the bunker. From the entrance one could reach the living rooms only through two so-called "locks" or compression chambers in the corridor. The locks must be seen as two antechambers that were separated from one another and from the corridor by armour-plated doors. Here Hitler's personal bodyguard was on duty. In the first corridor were the secretaries' bedrooms: Fräulein Wolf, Fräulein Schroeder, Frau Junge and Frau Christian ... From the first corridor there was a tortuous route to the second floor and the adjutants' rooms, those of Morell, Linge and the soldier servants. From here corridors went zigzagging towards Hitler's study and bedroom. Hitler's dining room and the storerooms were also to be found in his bedroom.'[20] Oxygen was fed through pipes into Hitler's bedroom from canisters situated in a ditch outside – Hitler refused to have them inside in case they exploded.

According to notes made by Heinrich Heim, Henry Picker and Martin Bormann, initially Hitler disliked his East Prussian headquarters: 'Here in the *Wolfsschanze*, I feel like a prisoner in these dugouts, and my spirit can't escape.

While Hitler may have had few luxuries in his bunker, as a field headquarters it was far from being unpleasant. Here we see him in his *arbeitszimmer*, his workroom or study, with Croatian Marshal Slavko Kvaternik in July 1941. As can be seen, this room had only partial wooden panelling, the walls above having been plastered and whitewashed.

Winter at the *Wolfsschanze*. This photograph, taken in February 1942, shows Hitler escorting the Romanian leader Ion Antonescu.

In my youth I dreamed constantly of vast spaces, and life has enabled me to give the dream reality. Ah, if we were at least in Berlin! Space lends wings to my imagination. Often I go at night to the card-room, and there I pace to and fro. In that way I get ideas.'[21]

But the longer Hitler stayed at the *Wolfsschanze*, the longer he felt at home there. Indeed, as news from the war fronts became increasingly bleak, Hitler developed something of a 'bunker mentality'. According to Dr Morell: 'It was the only place he felt at home: the only place he got the climate he liked (thanks to an air conditioning system) and the only place he could think and work.'[22] Smoking was not permitted in Hitler's bunker under any circumstances.

The working day and leisure time of the people in Hitler's headquarters were uncompromisingly subordinated to the Führer's needs and habits. Hitler's daily routine usually started in the morning around 10.00 hours after Hitler had been woken by his servant Heinz Linge. After breakfast, which consisted mostly of a glass of warm milk, rye or crispbread, and later oatmeal or muesli, and was conveyed by dumb waiter to Hitler's bedroom, he was given excerpts to read from newspapers previously selected by Ribbentrop. He received his mail at 10.30 hours. There was a daily air courier service between the Reich Chancellery in Berlin and the *Wolfsschanze*. All the

The *Führerbunker* was the largest single building in the *Wolfsschanze*.

documents that were presented to him were on one special typewriter that had extra-large letters. Since Hitler was near-sighted, everything had to be capitalised so that he could read it without glasses. He used a magnifying glass or glasses to look at maps.

After accepting the morning reports from all the battle fronts, Hitler would take a walk around the grounds, usually with his German shepherd bitch, Blondi, who would be taken to the Führerbunker by Hitler's dog handler. On Hitler's morning stroll no one dared to address him without a compelling reason; the area around the bunker where he walked being kept clear of any other persons. His doctors insisted that the Führer undertook this daily walk undisturbed for his health and stressed the importance of interacting with his dog Blondi during these walks to help him relax. According to Albert Speer, Hitler was usually more interested in playing with Blondi than any persons that might have been asked to accompany him.

Blondi performing one of her impressive feats in the snow at the *Wolfsschanze*.

Walter Baasch, who described himself as an 'ordinary' soldier, joined the *Führer-Begleit-Bataillon* and was transferred to the *Wolfsschanze* in the autumn of 1942. One day he was tasked with guarding Hitler on his morning walk. He had to keep his eyes on the Führer at all times but remain out of sight of Hitler, who did not like being watched, on what was his only break from the pressures of the war. During this duty, Baasch had the opportunity to see how the Führer played with Blondi. He would throw a stick for the dog to retrieve and then send her over various 'obstacles'; Blondi was able to balance on a pole, jump a 2m-high wall and climb a ladder.

At some point, possibly in early 1942, the *Wolfsschanze* acquired a cat, called Peter. Hitler had said that he did not like cats because they try to catch birds, but eventually he warmed to the animal and would be jealous if the cat chose someone else's lap to sit on.

Christa Schroeder detailed her daily routine at the *Wolfsschanze*. In the morning the secretaries had to wait in Dining Room I for Hitler to emerge from the conference room (what she termed the map room) after receiving the latest report on the situation at the front, when Hitler would sometimes join his secretaries for breakfast.

All the Führer ate on those occasions when he took his breakfast in the dining room was a glass of milk and a peeled apple. His secretaries, on the other hand, would eat as much food as they could get, even 'deftly' swapping their soiled cutlery for unused ones to gain a second helping of the sparse allowance.

In an annex to the right of the bunker was Hitler's personal kitchen. Hitler was a strict vegetarian and he used to mock those who did not share this conviction as 'corpse eaters'. He had a persistent fear of being poisoned and all vegetables and fruits prepared for the Führer were, where practicable, grown on the Berghof estate under close supervision. When Hitler was at the *Wolfsschanze*, these foodstuffs were flown into Rastenburg, with bread and similar products coming from Himmler's SS bakeries. Some products were purchased locally, but this was a security nightmare, plus it meant breaching the strict rationing regulations enforced throughout the Reich and Hitler, with his frugal lifestyle, would never for one moment contemplate this.[23]

Regardless of these measures, Hitler's food was subjected to the examination of a team of food-tasters before being passed on to the Führer. One of those who worked for the *Wolfsschanze* was Margot Woelk, who went to live with her in-laws in Gross Parsch, just 6 miles from Rastenburg, after being forced to leave her apartment in Berlin when the roof of the building was torn off by an RAF bomb one night in 1942. Within a week of her arrival at Gross Parsch she was on Hitler's payroll as a food taster. 'We boarded a bus with these S.S. thugs on board and drove to a house 11km away and there were fourteen other young women around my age there, all from the locality, all Germans.' Margot told an interviewer on her ninety-fifth birthday in

Hitler in the map room in April 1942, with Keitel and von Rundstedt.

An indication of the often relaxed atmosphere of the *Wolfsschanze* can possibly be gleaned from this scene, where a dining table sits in the open with what appears to be two or three empty wine glasses.

Two views of the inside of the *Führerbunker*.

December 2012. 'You will eat the dishes which have been prepared for the Führer and his staff each day between 11.00 am and noon before it is served,' the girls were told by what Margot called an SS adjutant.

'And that became my job. I felt like a lab rabbit. But if you learned one thing about life in Nazi Germany, it was that you didn't argue with the S.S.' Because of rationing, Margot had become used to a very paltry diet and she was delighted with the fare put before her: 'The food was simply wonderful. The freshest of vegetables, the best fruit. I shoved to the back of my mind that it might be poisoned because it all tasted so nice. Besides, there were so many checkpoints around the area, and so many S.S. men supervising everything, I failed to see how someone could sneak in and poison him. I remember no meat or fish, just vegetables.

'We all sat, all of us girls, around a big table and we each received a plateful of what was being served that day. There was asparagus in season once with a wonderful Hollandaise sauce I remember. Then there were vegetable broths with little semolina dumplings, roasted red peppers, rice, salads, and vegetable stews once a week – the so called "one pot meals" which the Reich asked all its citizens to eat at least once a week. It wasn't like we were given a spoonful or a forkful. We were given plates of the stuff to eat.

'Only after we had eaten did the S.S. commander of the day give instructions for the food to be boxed up and driven over to the compound inside the Wolf's Lair. And this was my life, five days a week.'[24]

Margot also remembered that there was also a noticeable change in the atmosphere in the *Wolfsschanze* after the 20 July 1944 assassination attempt: 'Things changed for us girls overnight. Until then I had spent every night with my in-laws, but the paranoia of Hitler now demanded that we would become virtual prisoners.

'We were shipped off to an empty school building and put into dormitory beds and only allowed to go home at weekends. We were guarded by S.S. the whole time and they were really jittery.'

Hitler also had a dietician at the *Wolfsschanze*, Helene Marie von Exner, who was brought to the headquarters by Doctor Morell. She was Austrian, from Vienna, and had been a dietician at Vienna University Hospital when she was offered a position in the service of Marshal Ion Antonescu, the Prime Minister and Conducător of Romania.[25] The Romanian leader had stomach problems, which he hoped to control by diet. This apparently worked after just a few months, and when Antonescu met Hitler in the spring of 1943, and the subject of their conversation turned to their respective delicate digestive systems, Antonescu told of his dietary success. Predictably, the Führer then told Morell to find him a dietician. Morell, with some reluctance, believing that his medicines alone were able to help Hitler, hired Frau von Exner. She received a tax-free salary of 800 Reichsmark a month, plus bonuses if her food helped Hitler avoid the stomach cramps that so often troubled him.

Being Austrian helped smooth the relationship between Hitler and Frau Exner. The stories she told him of her family life in Vienna amused the Führer and the two became friends. Soon she was cooking all of Hitler's meals and was given what Traudl Junge described as 'a special little diet kitchen built next to the main kitchen for the mess'. This, presumably, means next to Dining Room I, but the remains of that little kitchen have long since disappeared. Helene Exner was able to vary Hitler's rather bland diet, cooking vegetarian soups, and was even able to serve Viennese pastries after his stew of carrots with potatoes and hard-boiled eggs. The vegetables and fruit used in Hitler's meals were from a garden created nearby at what is now Mazurolandia amusement park. According to another of the food tasters, Margot Wölk, Hitler's meals were then made of 'the most delicious fresh things from asparagus to peppers and peas, served with rice and salads'. Situated just under a kilometre to the east, the garden has recently been uncovered. Unfortunately for Helene, it was later found that she had a Jewish grandmother and she was dismissed from Hitler's service in May 1944.

Continuing with the description of the daily routine at the *Wolfsschanze*, after breakfast, the secretaries had to listen to the Führer explain the current state of the war before, at 13.00 hours, they all went into the map room to hear the general situation report, which was usually given by Oberst Schmundt or Major Engel. This was followed by lunch, which was served in Dining Room (*Kasino*) I promptly at 14.00 hours. Fraulein Schroeder described the dining room, which had seats for twenty people at one of the two tables and chairs for six at the second table, as: 'an elongated white-painted room set quite deep in the ground so that the small gauze-covered windows are quite high up. The walls are decorated with marquetry ... A few days after moving in, a captured Soviet flag was fixed to the wall ... The boss [Hitler] seats himself so that he can gaze at the map of Russia on the opposite wall, which naturally spurs him into new monologues about Soviet Russia and the dangers of Bolshevism.'[26]

Hitler usually sat in the same place with his back to the windows, to his right sat Press Chief Dr Otto Dietrich and to his left was Generaloberst Alfred Jodl, Directly opposite the Führer was Keitel, to his right was Bormann opposite sat General Karl-Heinrich Bodenschatz. If there were any guests, they would sit between Hitler and Dietrich.

There, the meal usually consisted of stew – often of peas and beans – or soup, followed by meat and dessert. Hitler's own special menu was drawn up by himself at breakfast time. According to Nicolaus von Below, who was Hitler's long-serving Luftwaffe adjutant, the atmosphere at lunch times was free and unforced: 'Conversation was spontaneous and there was no kind of compulsion about what could be discussed. On subjects of general interest, when Hitler contributed his opinion silence would be maintained. It occurred occasionally that he would hold the floor, so as to speak, for up to an hour, but this was the exception to the rule. The extended mealtimes often forced many younger diners to excuse themselves from table for duty. Hitler never took this the wrong way.'[27]

There were occasions when there were changes to the usual simple fare, particularly Christmas and Hitler's birthday on 20 April. On his first birthday at the *Wolfsschanze* in 1942, Hitler welcomed a number of guests, including Göring, Ribbentrop and Admiral Raeder. The dining room was set out with tablecloths and flowers and the event was celebrated with cups of real coffee and glasses of German wine.[28]

For the grossly underworked secretaries, the afternoon was normally one of relaxation; they were even able to have a nap to prepare themselves for the rest of the day, which generally lasted well into the small hours. Then, towards 17.00 hours, the women were expected to re-join Hitler for coffee and cakes, with the Führer encouraging the women to indulge themselves, with the one that ate the most receiving praise from Hitler. Though their duties were few, Hitler enjoyed the company of his female secretaries, and the coffee 'hour' would frequently last until 19.00 or even later.

Hitler's relationship with women was, seemingly, quite a normal one. He was certainly very close to Eva Braun. Eva never visited the *Wolfsschanze*, staying when he was away in the east of Germany either in Munich or at the Berghof. He used to phone her every day from the *Wolfsschanze* and if he could not get hold of her he used to 'pace relentlessly like a caged lion, waiting to get in touch'.

After coffee it was then back to the dining room for dinner, followed by a walk around the grounds or the women would watch a film in the cinema to kill time until tea, after which the party would wander back to the conference room for the evening situation report.

Hitler took his tea in his study, where a round table with rattan chairs stood before a large fireplace. Traudl Junge has left us a detailed account of Hitler's study at the time before the final building stage at the *Wolfsschanze*. On one side there were five large windows that fully lit the room, framed by colourfully printed 'rustic-style' curtains. Almost the whole of this wall was taken up by a long, broad table covered with maps and where several telephones, desk lamps and pencils stood. Hitler's desk occupied much of the remaining space. It was, according to the secretary, 'an ordinary oak desk, the kind you get in any modern office'.[29]

Many of the military conferences took place in the dining room. It was also where regular guests, such as Hitler's doctor, Theodor Morell, his military and personal adjutants, Martin Bormann and his adjutant, Heinrich Heim, and the two secretaries, would sit and talk, or listen to Hitler's views.[30]

There was, it seems, little point in anything other than listening to Hitler, as stenographer Dr Ewald Reynitz would later recall: 'The most striking feature was how Hitler actually dominated everybody around him, not by bullying but simply talking, talking and talking. There was never such a thing as might be called discussions, only monologue after monologue. Göring sometimes would start contradicting, but his arguments were mostly so poor that Hitler simply waved them aside. Jodl was the only one who in fact spoke up.'[31]

Benito Mussolini, the Italian fascist leader, found himself subject to one of Hitler's monologues during a well-publicised visit to the *Wolfsschanze* in August 1941. At that stage of the war, hopes were still high of success against the Soviets and Hitler welcomed Mussolini enthusiastically. Il Duce arrived by train and he was met by Hitler at the *Wolfsschanze* station. Immediately the Führer began extolling the achievements of the German forces and for the rest of the day, the weary Mussolini was barely able to open his mouth. Hitler talked unceasingly for hours about the forthcoming victory until the Italian leader could not bear to hear any more about German glory and butted in to relate the triumphs of ancient Rome.

The evening discussions at the *Wolfsschanze* often went on for hours, as Christa Schroeder explained in a letter on 13 July 1941: 'The sessions last a ridiculously long time and one is by then – if not actually ready to drop – at least so enervated and bereft of energy … The night before last when we left him it was dawn. Instead of going to bed as normal people do we had a couple of sandwiches in the kitchen and then went for a two-hour run direct into the sunrise. Past horses and cattle in corrals, past hills of red and white clover simply fabulous in the morning sun. I could not get enough of it. Then we went to bed and spent three hours exhausted, unable to bestir ourselves. A mad existence, don't you think?'[32]

This relaxed atmosphere changed markedly after Hitler dismissed Generalfeldmarschall von Brauchitsch from his position as head of the Heer and the Führer took over operational command of the army. The extra workload that Hitler had taken on meant that the previous daily routine was rarely adhered to. Lunch was sometimes taken as late as 18.00 hours and the tea sessions did not start until after midnight at the conclusion of the evening situation conference, which was scheduled to begin at 21.00 or 22.00 hours. These teatime chats sometimes ended with Hitler falling asleep through exhaustion, and those in the tearoom (which Walter Dornberger said was 'simply and tastefully furnished') having to sit in silence to avoid waking their boss.

At the evening sessions stretched farther into the night, so Hitler remained in his bedroom ever later, often not rising until midday. Speer remarked caustically that if that trend continued, the whole routine would go full circle around the clock until it was back at the original time.

Another rare view inside Hitler's study, with its simple furnishings as described by Traudl Junge. The person in this photograph being received by Hitler is the Japanese ambassador, Baron Hiroshi Ōshima. Various sources give the date as 4 September 1944.

The front of Hitler's bunker survived the demolition efforts in fairly good order, possibly helped by the fact that the foundations of the building reached 7m into the ground.

In its final, massive form, Hitler's bunker measured some 200ft long and 120ft wide, surrounded by 23ft of concrete divided by a layer of basalt to act as a shock absorber if the building was struck by a bomb.

There are two other structures on the left side of the road (to the north) opposite the *Führerbunker*. The first of these is **Building No. 12**, which was a small flak bunker (or *Flakstande*).

By the side of the Flak Bunker was a fire water reservoir, **Building No. 14**.

Continuing on the red route, there used to be a track, some 50m beyond the *Führerbunker*, which led to Lake Moysee to allow staff to go to the bathing area on the shores of the lake. This had long been a popular and highly frequented recreational spot for the people of Rastenburg. It had a bathing jetty with a diving platform, a wooden refreshment pavilion, a toilet and changing rooms, but only a small air-raid shelter was made for bathers. It had a good sandy beach, but this was inhabited by numerous leeches. Locals from Rastenburg, mainly young women, managed to find a way of getting to the beach despite the travel and security restrictions, and could also be seen swimming in the lake during the summer from June onwards.

The next object for visitors to investigate on the red route are the scant remains of Dining Room (*Kasino*) I, with little other to see than sections of its walls with tiles attached. This is **Building D**. The kitchen here was run by head chef Otto Günter from the Kaiserhof hotel in Berlin.

The flak bunker would have been manned by the *Führer-Flak-Abteilung*. This building also served as an emergency air-raid shelter before Hitler's bunker was reinforced in the 1944 redevelopment.

A close-up of what was probably one of the gun mounts on the roof of the Flak Bunker.

Building No. 14.

The fire water reservoir (or *löschwasserbecken*) was placed near Hitler's bunker in case of emergencies.

Diarist Helmuth Greiner wrote disparagingly about *Kasino* I in his diary, declaring that: 'it has an exceptionally nasty dining room that couldn't compete with even the ugliest village pub.'[33] It was described by Christa Schroder as 'a whitewashed room sunk half-underground, so that gauze covered windows are high up. A table for twenty people takes up the entire length of the room.' It can be found by the path that leads to Hitler's bunker almost directly in front of the entrance to the *Führerbunker*.[34]

Next to *Kasino* I was the New Teahouse. Albert Speer wrote approvingly: 'Its furnishings were a pleasant change from the general drabness. Here we occasionally met for a glass of vermouth; here field marshals waited before conferring with Hitler. He himself avoided this teahouse and thus escaped encounters with the generals and staff officers of the High Command and of the armed forces.'[35]

There is another junction here opposite which is a zigzag-shaped building. This is **Building No. 20** which was that of Wehrmacht Adjutant to the Führer and Chief of the Personnel Department of the German Army (Chefadiutanturen der Wehrmacht beim Führer), Leiter Heerespersonalamt. The man who was the head of the Personnel Department was Generalleutnant Rudolf Schumundt, and he was in the situation conference room at the time of the 20 July assassination attempt, where he was seriously injured and subsequently died of his wounds.

The scant remains of Dining Room I can be seen directly opposite Hitler's bunker across the path that runs along the back of the bunker shown in this photograph.

Detail of the white tiles on the collapsed walls of *Kasino* I.

Building No. 20.

Also, in Building No. 20, were the living quarters of Hitler's personal adjutants, Julius Schaub and Otto Günsche, when not on duty with the Führer. The building is in a very collapsed condition and its original size and shape is hard to visualise.

The right-hand fork marks the start of the yellow route, which merely takes visitors back to the car park, passing on their right the bunker or air-raid shelter of the Reich Press Secretary, Dr Otto Dietrich. Dietrich, who was awarded the Iron Cross in the First World War, received a doctorate in political science and began a career in the newspaper industry after the war before joining the Nazi Party in 1929 as a Personal Press Referent. In August of that year he was made the party's Press Chief and shortly after Hitler had become Chancellor, Dietrich, described by Traudl Junge as having 'a very mousy look and made a totally innocuous, insignificant, colourless impression' was, nevertheless, appointed Reich Press Secretary. While not regarded as one of the leading Nazis, his influence was considerable, being the man who put Hitler's often random ideas into intelligible language and, along with Goebbels, projected the desired public image of the Third Reich to the world.

As mentioned earlier, Alfons Schultz, who spent three years at the *Wolfsschanze*, worked in the press centre. He recalled how most found life in the *Wolfsschanze* dull and rules and procedures monotonous: 'All the inhabitants of *Wolfsschanze* tried in one way or another to escape the monotony of this life. For many, especially those who are not of the higher rank, this was mostly only possible with the beginning of spring on an expanded scale. They could again walk through the beautiful forests around Rastenburg or ride horses that they borrowed from the neighbouring country estates. The many lakes in the immediate vicinity, especially the Moy and Tauchel lakes, offered opportunities for boat trips, but also for fishing.'

The left fork continues along the red route to Generalfeldmarschall Wilhelm Keitel's bunker (**Building No. 19**). Until the autumn of 1942, all the main situation conferences held in *Sperrkreis* I took place in a large room in the *Keitelbunker*. The corresponding room in Hitler's bunker was set aside for small-scale conferences.

Keitel was one of the officers that survived the 20 July assassination attempt. He sat on the Army 'court of honour' in the investigations into the Army officers involved, or suspected to be involved, handing many of them over to the notorious People's Court. Keitel, as deputy supreme commander of the German armed forces (Oberster Befehlshaber der Wehrmacht), was the man who signed the German surrender document that brought the war in Europe to an end after Hitler's suicide.

To the north-east of Keitel's bunker are the remains of the Old Teahouse (**Building E**).

The red route then branches eastwards off the main road along a smaller track, which leads to the huge **Building No. 16**. Situated at the eastern extremity of *Sperrkreis* I, this is the Luftwaffe's command bunker, the *Luftschutzbunker*. It is in a severely collapsed state, although the roof is fairly intact. This is, according to Peter Hoffman, because the concrete of the ceiling of the bunker had been poured after the rest of the structure had already been

Building No. 19 was Keitel's bunker.

This photograph by Hoffmann taken on 10 August 1943 shows Hitler with Göring and Speer walking down the path from Hitler's bunker to that of Keitel.

Above and below, five photographs from inside Keitel's bunker. Keitel was the most senior military officer at the *Wolfsschanze*.

The steel girders that supported the roof.

The metal frame of what was once a doorway.

Electrical wires were neatly concealed within the walls, but this was not always the case. In order to have everything ready for the start of Operation *Barbarossa*, the work was rushed, and in some instances, the electrical cables were simply laid over the plaster of the walls. Many metres of installation ducts had to be chiselled into the finished reinforced concrete ceilings and walls at considerable effort as they had been overlooked during construction.

The remains of the Old Teahouse, the *Altes Teehaus*.

It is difficult to visualize the exact shape of the Old Teahouse due to its ruinous state.

This photograph was taken by Heinrich Hoffmann in the New Tearoom in the summer of 1943. Albert Speer, in his role of Reich Minister for Armaments and Ammunition, is being presented with the Fritz-Todt-Ring of Deutsche Technik in a plaque with a portrait of Dr Fritz Todt in a decorated silver box for the extraordinary increase in the production of weapons, tanks and ammunition in the previous year.

built and only shortly before its destruction in January 1945. Consequently, the ceiling and the walls had not fully bonded when the demolition charges went off. As a result, the explosion blew the roof into the air and as it dropped back, it fell on to the weak bunker walls.[36]

The road then swings around to the east along what was the perimeter of *Sperrkreis* I and parallel to the railway line. There, immediately behind the *Luftschutzbunker* is Göring's personal house, the *Reichsmarschalhause* (**Building No. 15**). Despite the grandeur of this brick-built structure – and what was effectively his personal air-raid shelter – Göring spent most of his time in East Prussia as his own *Hauptquartier Robinson*, which is described further on in this guide. Göring did, however, move into the *Reichsmarschalhause* in October 1944 when he was compelled to abandon *Robinson* as the Red Army advanced towards Germany.

Göring's first visit to the *Wolfsschanze*, a few days after Hitler had arrived, was a momentous one. This was because the following day the Führer signed a secret decree confirming Göring as his exclusive successor in the event of his own death, and as his 'deputy in all offices'.

Building No. 16.

The buckled walls of the *Luftschutzbunker* where the massive roof fell on to them during its destruction in 1945.

The collapsed condition of the *Luftschutzbunker*.

Much of the interior of the *Luftschutzbunker* is still surprisingly intact.

One of the entrances to No. 16. In October 1944, Göring had to abandon his *Robinson* complex as Soviet forces advanced on East Prussia. He transferred to the *Wolfsschanze* and remained there until the site was abandoned in November of that year.

The external ladder to the top of No. 16. There are no restrictions regarding using the ladder to access the roof.

The climb up to the top of No. 16.

Above and below are photographs of the roof of the *Luftschutzbunker*, where there were two anti-aircraft guns, one machine gun and one searchlight position.

As well as one of the anti-aircraft gun mounts, this photograph also shows the eyelets used to tie the camouflage netting.

The rooftop entrance/exit to the *Luftschutzbunker*'s internal ladder.

A postcard from the early post-war period provides a good view of the gun positions on top of the *Luftschutzbunker*.

The *Luftschutzbunker* in 1944 with Göring's *Reichsmarschalhause* behind it.

Though building No. 16 is shown in the background of this meeting between Hitler and Sepp Dietrich in August 1944, the number refers to its wartime identification. This is in fact Building O (see below).

Building No. 15.

Despite the swampy nature of the ground, Göring's house appears to have had a basement.

The basement is flooded with water, demonstrating why most of the *Wolfsschanze* buildings were erected predominately above ground.

Inside Göring's residence.

Göring's once luxurious accommodation now lies in ruins.

Continuing south, the route travels to what was the eastern entrance to the *Wolfsschanze*, *Wache Ost*. Here it is possible to cross the railway line. This leads to a road running east to west, and a left turn takes the visitor to a field that was used as an airfield for short take-off Fieseler Storch liaison aircraft. There was also a command building, or control tower, here.

To return to the red route, it is necessary to retrace the road back to Göring's residence. From there, travelling westwards can be found **Building No. 17**, which was the bunker of Generaloberst Alfred Jodl, who was Chief of the Operations Staff of the *Oberkommando der Wehrmacht*. Jodl spent most of the war at the *Wolfsschanze*.

The next building along is **Building No. 18**, which was *Kasino* or Dining Room II. This was, effectively, the officers' mess and was one of the few buildings that had a basement, in this case a wine cellar. Hitler tended to keep away from *Kasino* II to avoid having to discuss the progress of the war with officers who might be present.

The red route now leads to the vehicle compound and the previously mentioned Building No. 22, the garage. Also facing the compound was a telephone/teleprinter exchange, the *Nachrichtenbunker* or news centre bunker (**Building No. 21**). Responsibility for the installation and housing of the

The Storch airfield.

Building No. 17.

Inside Jodl's bunker.

Building No. 17 with No. 18 in the distance.

Building No. 18.

Inside Building No. 18.

Both No. 17 and No. 18 were classed as heavy Type A bunkers.

Almost opposite Building No. 18 is **Building F**, a chimney for a heating plant (*heizhaus*).

telecommunications equipment, as well as its maintenance, was the role of the 314-strong *Stabssignalskompanie*. Telecommunications were handled by the *Führer-Nachrichtenabetabteilung*.

The maintenance of the communications system in general was in the hands of the Reichspost, whereas the actual operation of the main telephone exchange for all the headquarters in the region associated with the *Wolfsschanze*, which was at Allenstein (present-day Olsztyn) and code-named *Annabu*, was controlled by the OKH. There was also an independent telegraphy unit at Heligenlinde (Święta Lipka), some 22km to the west of the *Wolfsschanze*.[37]

Through means of a sophisticated encryption system, direct contact with the commanders in the field as well as with the military and civil services in Berlin, or their respective locations, was possible at any time. Telephone, telex and radio connections could be established to all parts of the armed forces right down to the forward posts on all fronts, including North Africa. German embassies in friendly foreign countries could also be reached with just a brief delay.

A team of twelve men manned the network twenty-four hours a day on a three-shift rota, with six men manning the telephones and three specialists for each of the radio and telex services. All calls, except for those of the Führer, were recorded on magnetic tape.

Each day the men on the morning shift began work at 08.00 hours, taking over from the night shift, the latter going to bed at 08.30 after breakfast. Meanwhile, those on the afternoon shift had to clean the barracks, this chore having to be completed by 08.15 hours. Their shift began at 14.00 hours. Once a week these procedures were shortened by an hour and a 'cleaning and mending hour' was inserted instead. In addition to this, every Saturday there was a big cleaning of the rooms. Copious amounts of water were carried to the barracks hut in buckets and the floors sluiced down, a floorboard being removed to allow the water to drain away quickly.

One of those who worked in the telecommunications bunker was Karl Otto Wendel who, along with the other staff, was accommodated in *Sperrkreis* II: 'The modest equipment of the barrack included bunk wooden beds, wardrobes, tables, stools and radio. We went to zone 1 for work. Each of us had a special pass, which was often exchanged ... The communications bunker was a windowless building and consisted of three departments: On one side of the building there were radiotelegraphic services, telephones on the other, and a telephone exchange inside. The latter was divided into three boxes: Each of them had 150 disconnection sockets. The middle box in which I operated, served the most important connections. ... The internal rooms of the communications bunker were entered through three metal doors spaced a few meters apart. The rooms between the doors served as air chambers. Although the shelter was ventilated with the help of fans, the rooms felt unpleasant

Building No. 21.

Another view of the telecommunications bunker, No. 21. All the buildings in the *Wolfsschanze* differed from one another in their size, size of the rooms, and the strength of the double walls and ceilings. Even those classed as standard Luftwaffe barracks were arranged differently inside depending on their purpose.

stuffy. Those who worked here for a long time suffered from cardiovascular disease. Smoking was also popular and excessive drinking of black coffee too. We received coffee, as well as excellent food, good wines and cognacs from the casino staff and some important personalities of the Wolf's Lair, who in this way repaid us for private, in principle prohibited phone calls to their friends or families.'[38]

Wendel said that he handled the communications of Göring and Keitel among others, but that every conversation was subordinate to those of Hitler, which were carried out by what he called two special coding devices or 'inverters', most probably what is now known as Enigma machines. The codes for the machines were changed each day, being delivered by special Reichspost couriers.

Also facing this compound was the cinema, or *kino* (**Building H**). This played a vital role in the social life of the *Wolfsschanze*. For many, used to the vibrant nightlife of Berlin, the 'horrid ... dirty green, gloomy, airless forest encampment ... permanently swathed in fog', as one resident described it, was excruciatingly dull, and apart from drinking and conversation there was little else to keep the residents entertained other than the cinema. Films were shown at 20.15 and 22.15 hours every night, although the exact timings were determined by the senior man in Dining Room I. Every Friday at 17.00 newsreels were shown, among which were Pathé news scenes from the bombing of London. As the cinema was a wooden building, smoking was not permitted.

As time progressed, the residents, having watched every available current film, were reduced to watching old silent movies. Hitler encouraged visitors to use the cinema, but he did not attend himself, preferring to watch films in his own quarters, and he saw all the German newsreels – the *Deutsche Wochenschau* – before they were allowed to be shown in the cinema, which he carefully censored. These were silent films and, according to one of Hitler's valets, Karl Wilhelm Krause, one of the adjutants would read out loud the accompanying text with Hitler checking that the words fitted the film footage. Often, he dictated what he thought needed to be corrected. From the winter of 1942 onwards, Hitler stopped watching the newsreels.[39]

There was, though, one special evening in the cinema that Hitler attended. This was when Generalmajor Walter Dornberger, head of the Army Weapons Department, was invited on 7 July 1943 to give a presentation on the A4 rocket, which later became the feared V2 that so terrorised London the following year. Dornberger wrote of that memorable day as his aircraft flew beyond the River Vistula and as the skies cleared, 'below us, as far as the eye could see, stretched the dark forests of East Prussia, plentifully adorned with glittering lakes and occasionally flower-decked meadows'.

The viewing took place a little after 17.00 hours. Hitler entered the room escorted by Keitel and Alfred Jodl (who described the *Wolfsschanze* as 'a cross between a monastery and a concentration camp'). Dornberger was shocked at the deterioration in the Führer's appearance since he had last seen him, four years earlier: 'A voluminous black cape covered his bowed, hunched shoulders and bent back. He looked a tired man. Only the eyes retained their life. They stared from a face grown unhealthily pallid from living in huts and shelters and seemed to be all pupils.'[40]

With a commentary by a soon-to-be-professor Wernher von Braun, Hitler was shown astonishing film footage of the V2 rocket for the first time soaring majestically not just into the sky, but into space. The film ended and von Braun finished his commentary. 'No one dare utter a word,' continued Dornberger. 'Hitler was visibly moved and agitated. Lost in thought, he lay back in his chair, staring gloomily in front of him ... At last ... Hitler walked rapidly over to me and shook my hand ... If we had had these rockets in 1939,' said the Führer, 'we should never have had this war.'

Another film that Hitler allegedly watched (though probably in the confines of his own quarters) was the execution of eight of the senior figures involved in the 20 July 1944 assassination attempt. The film was shot in Plötzensee prison, Berlin, where the condemned men were stripped to the waist and hanged by nooses of piano wire attached to meat hooks suspended from the ceiling of the small prison room. The barbaric scene was played on 18 August at the *Wolfsschanze*. According to Albert Speer, 'Hitler loved the film and had it shown over and over again.'[41]

Dr Dietmar Pertsch recalled being in the cinema two days after Hitler's fifty-third birthday on 20 April 1942, when the weekly propaganda film, the main part of which was dedicated to the war in the East, was shown. This included three shots of Hitler's birthday celebrations. The first of these was a celebration of the NSDAP (the Nazi Party) on the eve of the birthday, which showed the 'national unity' with high party officials alongside wounded soldiers and war widows listening to the closing chorus from Beethoven's 9th Symphony with the Berlin Philharmonic conducted by Wilhelm Furtwängler. The middle section was a 'typical' Nazi weekly show with a lot of blaring trumpets and ordinary Germans meeting senior Reich figures, plus a group of children from Rastenburg singing gentle songs superimposed with an image of Hitler. The martial music returned followed by lots of smiling faces and a happy-looking Führer. The entire production had been carefully crafted by Goebbels as 'patron of the German film' and bore no relationship to the dreadful struggles of the German army battling deep inside Russia. Yet, as Dr Pertsch asked himself: 'Did we see through the dramatic concept? No! We were proud of ourselves to have been there in the *Wolfsschanze* and seen the Führer. I still hear one of my comrades, who had given a bouquet of flowers in his hand by Hitler, loudly exclaim "now I will never wash again because the Führer has shaken it!"'

While the Wehrmacht handled the telephone services, the RSD dealt with the mail as well as its main function of protecting Hitler and guarding *Sperrkreis* I. Rochus Misch of the RSD was Hitler's bodyguard, whose principal duty was to be within range of Hitler at all times and available for any tasks the Führer might require. He left the following description of his time at the *Wolfsschanze*, which gives the impression of a surprisingly relaxed atmosphere at what was a field headquarters at the height of the most destructive and barbaric military campaign in history: 'Nothing exciting happened, and the mood became generally more informal. To put it another way, we lazed around. Soon we sought to overcome our boredom by swimming in the nearby Moysee Lake. Civilians came there from the nearby villages to bathe. They had no worries about being disturbed by us. We took car trips ever further afield, into the glorious countryside. The lakes of the Masurian plateau and the beauty of the scenery enchanted me.

'In the evening we sat in our barrack hut and played cards … the room hazy with the cigarette smoke of my colleagues … when off duty, nearly all of my colleagues would puff away for all they were worth.

'Besides Hitler, we also had time to look after a young roe fawn, which came to us one day. We fed it peanuts, and the crafty animal soon knew exactly where we kept these and was soon helping itself. It would also come up the steps to the hut, push open the door with its snout and lick up the peanuts from the floor. We would leave the door open intentionally, and often the fawn would come up to our beds for assistance if it failed to find what it was looking for.'[42] It is hard to believe that it was from the *Wolfsschanze* that the most important conflict of the Second World War was being directed.

Across the road from the *Nachrichtenbunker* is **Building I**, which is given as being the accommodation block for 'Government and Service Liaison Officers, Doctors, Barbers, etc.'[43]

Traudl Junge related in her memoires her first visit to Hitler at the *Wolfsschanze* in 1943 accompanied by other young women who were being assessed for their suitability to serve the Führer in the role of secretary. From her account of the building they were taken to before their interview with Hitler, and her explanation of the route they took to Hitler's bunker, it could well be Building I: 'We passed through the low entrance into a narrow concrete corridor with a great many doors, almost like something in a big steamship, and went through the first door on the left into a waiting room. It measured about three metres by four and was used by both the domestic staff and Hitler's orderlies.'[44]

Building I.

Inside Building I.

Dr Theodor Morell's quarters were also in this building. He was the only person allowed the indulgence of a bath in his quarters, and a standard-size bath was duly installed at the *Wolfsschanze* for him. Doctor Morell, however, was a rather portly individual. He was just about able to get into his bath but could not get out without help! Predictably, he was the butt of many jokes in the confined atmosphere of the Wolf's Lair.

Morell was another who disliked the *Wolfsschanze*: 'The bunker is damp and unhealthy, the temperature is just right for growing fungi; once my boots were mouldy after being left two days, and my clothes got clammy in the bedroom. New bunker walls always sweat quantities of water at first. Everybody here's got rheumatism and aches and pains. Then there are the colds caused by the draught of the extractor fans. I pointed out all that after just four days in the bunker ... people got chest constrictions, anaemia, and general bunker psychosis.'[45]

Hitler's official photographer, Heinrich Hoffmann, also lived here: 'My own quarters were simple but well-founded and comfortable, consisting of a sitting-room, bedroom and bathroom, and, to help me to while away my many free hours, I was also given a wireless. In the same barracks with me lived Professor Dr Morell, Admiral Voss, General Bodenschatz, who was Göring's adjutant, and Obergruppenführer Wolf, Himmler's adjutant.'[46]

Heinrich Hoffmann congratulating Hitler on his birthday on 20 April 1943 at the *Wolfsschanze.*

Hoffmann said that his duties consisted exclusively of taking photographs of officers and men who had gone to the *Wolfsschanze* to be presented with medals that they had won. He wrote about his time at the *Wolfsschanze*, describing Hitler's 1944 bunker as, 'windowless and devoid of fresh air; night and day they were lighted by electricity, and a pump did its best to keep the atmosphere healthy'.

The red route continues past Building No. 22, where the road branches yet again. The right-hand fork lead leads back to the car park, whereas the left one runs over the railway line to the blue route.

Heading south across the railway line at *Wache Süd*, the blue route heads eastwards until opposite *Wache Ost*, where a turn to the right leads to **Building No. 24**, which was that of the liaison officers (or *verbindungsstab*) of the Air Force High Command, the Oberkommando der Luftwaffe (OKL), under Bodenschatz.

Heinz Kettner was a soldier with the Führer-Flak-Abteilung 12. Batterie in the *Wolfsschanze* from April 1944 to November 1944. He described his accommodation as being in a simple wooded barracks in *Sperrkreis* II that

Crossing the railway line.

Building No. 24.

Inside No. 24. As can be seen, some electrical light fittings still exist.

Behind the OKL building was the former cemetery of the village of Partsch, where the deceased villagers were buried until 1942, as can be seen from the inscriptions of the tombstones that have been preserved until today. No one that died in the *Wolfsschanze* was interred there.

was situated between Building No. 24 and the Storch air strip. It accommodated twenty men. They had to wash outside in the open air next to the barracks. His duty was to stand on guard for two hours, after which he was relieved for four hours before another two-hour stint. After ten days on duty he was granted one day off. He claims that he had to do this around the clock, all year round, but was granted one day off after ten days on duty. He would spend that day walking, hitch-hiking to Rastenburg or watching films in the cinema.[47]

Continuing southwards along this road, after about 50m on the left is **Building No. 25** of the former liaison staff of the Navy, the *Oberkommando der Marine* (OKM). This was under the command of Konteradmiral Hans-Erich Voss, as the Oberbefehlshaber der Marine's permanent representative at the FHQ.[48]

By taking the right turn at the intersection after No. 25, **Building No. 26** can be seen on the right-hand side of the road. This was the general air-raid shelter, or *Allgemeiner Luftschtzbunker*, for the whole of the *Wolfsschanze*.

The next building along this road, approximately 100m on the right, is **Building No. 27**. This was accommodation for the *Führer-Begleit-Bataillon*. The FBB was employed to guard Hitler's numerous *Führerhauptquartiere* (as well

Building No. 25.

Konteradmiral Voss and his team occupied two buildings on either side of the road, both of which constitute No. 25. This is the building on the right-hand side of the road.

Building No. 26.

Despite the enormous scale of this double bunker, the passages in No. 26 are very narrow.

The ladders to the roof are in excellent condition.

as the railway tracks used by the Führer's train), and to guard him on visits outside Germany. It was also the case that the troopers had to stand-to at the station every time a train passed along the railway line, even if it was not stopping at the *Wolfsschanze*.

In August 1943 the FBB was renamed the *Führer-Grenadier-Bataillon*. It was upgraded to the *Führer-Begleit-Regiment* in September 1944.

The weather in East Prussia, what is now northern Poland, is one of extremes, ranging from −7°C or even lower in the winter, to 24° or more in the summer. In and around the Görlitz forest were lakes and swamps that were the home to countless mosquitoes, which plagued the occupants of the *Wolfsschanze* throughout the summer, and, as warned earlier, continue to do so to visitors and workers today.

Gertraud 'Traudl' Humps was one of four secretaries eventually employed by Hitler and she wrote of her time at the *Wolfsschanze*, complaining that: 'Swarms of midges and mosquitoes hovered over the marshy meadows, making our lives a misery. The guards had to wear mosquito netting over their faces, and the windows were fitted with mesh to keep the flies out.' She was not impressed either, by the accommodation at the *Wolfsschanze*:

Building No. 27. The approximately 56m × 30m brick building was one of the few two-storey buildings within the complex.

This photograph of No. 27 shows how well concealed the buildings could be.

The steps leading to the upper floor of No. 27.

Inside No. 27.

As seen previously with the windows, the entrances, such as this one on No. 27, were secured by heavy steel doors, though now only the hinges remain.

'I exchanged my compartment in the special train for a little room in the secretaries' bunker, was given a permanent pass for the restricted area, and now I was living about a hundred metres from the Führer bunker itself. I wasn't entirely happy with my new quarters ... I was working in a room with small windows during the day, but I had to sleep in an uninviting, windowless little cell ... Air came through a ventilator in the ceiling. If you closed it you felt you were stifling, if you opened it the air wheezed noisily as it came into the little room, and you might have been sitting in an aeroplane.[49]

The noisy ventilation systems were frequently switched off by personnel throughout the complex, which caused dampness in the rooms. Nor was it usually possible to open any windows to allow the air in, unless the windows were carefully protected by mosquito nets. Poisoned fly-papers were hung inside the buildings, which proved effective in trapping the mosquitoes that had managed to fly inside.

At night, the forest was filled with the sound of croaking frogs that inhabited the swamps. One night, Hitler noticed that the frogs had gone silent. When he asked what had happened to the frogs, he was told that the mosquito plague had been dealt with. A few hundred litres of kerosene had been poured into the pools and had killed many thousands of mosquitoes but, unfortunately, it had also killed off the frogs.

Hitler was furious: 'Have you seen idiots like that?' he stormed. 'They got rid of the frogs, the mosquitoes stayed! The frogs catch thousands of mosquitoes every day.'

Under Hitler's instructions, the puddles contaminated with petroleum were painstakingly cleaned, fresh water was poured in and the frogs returned. But because the mosquitoes have a much shorter reproduction cycle, they were able to repopulate the area much quicker and they continued to torment the unfortunate residents of the *Wolfsschanze*.

Helmuth Greiner, who did not like the *Wolfsschanze* at all, complained that: 'We're being plagued by the most awful mosquitoes. It would be hard to pick on a more senseless site than this – deciduous forest with marshy pools, sandy ground, and stagnant lakes, ideal for these loathsome creatures. On top of which, our bunkers are cold and damp. We freeze to death at night, can't get to sleep because of the humming of the air conditioning and the terrible draught it makes, and we wake up every morning with a headache. Our underwear and uniforms are always cold and clammy.'[50] According to one authority, Hitler later agreed with Greiner, grumbling that: 'No doubt some government department found the land was cheapest here.'[51] Hitler's disenchantment with the location of the *Wolfsschanze* can hardly have been improved when, on 7 August 1941, he was very ill for a number of days with bacillary dysentery, which Dr Morell said was from the surrounding swamplands.

Another of Hitler's secretaries, Christa Schroeder, was ambivalent about the *Wolfsschanze* when she first settled in there in the summer of 1941: 'Our dormitory bunker is the size of a railway compartment and has light-coloured wood panelling. There is a discreet washbasin, above it a mirror, a small Siemens radio with a wide choice of stations. The bunker even has electric heating, not yet connected up, eye-catching wall lamps and a narrow hard mattress filled with eel-grass. The room is narrow but all in all it will have a nice look once I have hung a few pictures. Common shower rooms are available, but until now we have not used them. At first there was no hot water ... Because the noise from the fan in the bunker disturbed us and the draught passed continuously above our heads, which I hate especially because of the rheumatic pains I so often have, we requested that it be turned off at night with the consequence that we now sleep in a fug and suffer all next day from a leaden heaviness in the limbs.'[52]

Schroeder, like everyone at the *Wolfsschanze*, hated the mosquitoes, which she called 'midges': 'I have midge bites all up my legs which are now covered in thick swellings. The anti-midge precautions last us only a short while. The men have better protection than we do (long leather boots and thick uniforms). Their only vulnerable spot is the neck. Some wear a mosquito net all the time.'

Hitler's bunker before its concrete reinforcement of 1944. The entrance was shielded by the wire grids shown here to prevent mosquitos entering the building.

The wood panelling described by Christa Schroeder and others is clearly seen in the following photographs. The first of these shows the Italian Foreign Minister, Galeazzo Ciano, being greeted by Hitler during an official visit to the *Wolfsschanze* on 18 December 1942.

The second view of the wooden panelling shows the Commander of the Spanish Volunteer Division on the Eastern Front, Lieutenant General Augustin Munoz-Grandes (left), at the *Wolfsschanze* being presented with the Knight's Cross of the Iron Cross with Oakleaves by Hitler on 16 December 1942. Munoz-Grandes was the Commander of the so-called 'Blue Division' establishment during the Russian campaign.

In this third view of the panelling, wooden flooring can be seen that was typical of the *Wolfsschanze* buildings. In this photograph, the Hungarian Armed Forces Minister, General Vitéz Lajos Csatay de Csataj (left), is talking with Hitler during an official visit to the *Wolfsschanze* on 24 November 1943.

On 19 June 1943, Traudl Humps married Hitler's valet and orderly Obersturmführer Hans Hermann Junge. After just four weeks, Junge joined the Waffen-SS and Traudl resumed her secretarial duties, describing in her memoirs the nature of the *Wolfsschanze* at that time: 'The forest had been cleared around it to make room for several more huts and bunkers. What we called 'hut disease' had broken out and proved very infectious among the upper ranks. Everyone wanted his own hut to live in, and the bunkers were only used for sleeping. Speer built himself a whole housing estate. Göring's hut was nothing short of a palace.'[53]

Albert Speer took over Fritz Todt's position as Minister of Armaments and Munitions following Todt's fatal air crash at Rastenburg. Ironically, Speer had arrived at the *Wolfsschanze* the evening before the crash and had accepted Todt's offer to fly with him to Berlin. Speer cancelled some hours before take-off because the previous night he had been up late in a meeting with Hitler.

Speer later wrote about that visit – his first – to the *Wolfsschanze*. He was on his way back to Berlin from Ukraine and was offered the chance to visit the Führerhauptquartiere. After landing at Rastenburg, he was driven to the *Wolfsschanze* in one of Hitler's cars: 'There I had a good meal in the dining barracks where Hitler ate daily with his generals, political associates, and adjutants. Hitler himself was not present. Dr Todt … was reporting to him, and the two were dining alone in Hitler's private apartment … It was late at night before Todt emerged, strained and fatigued … By chance he mentioned … that he was to fly back to Berlin next morning and that there was an unoccupied seat in his plane. He said he would be glad to take me along, and I was relieved not to have to make that long trip by rail. We agreed to fly at an early hour, and Dr Todt bade me goodnight, since he was going to try to get a little sleep.

'An adjutant came in and requested me to join Hitler. It was then after one o'clock in the morning; in Berlin, too, we had often sat over our plans at this hour. Hitler seemed as exhausted and out of sorts as Todt. The furniture of his room stressed sparseness; he had even renounced the comfort of an upholstered chair here at headquarters. … When I finally left Hitler at three o'clock in the morning, I sent word that I would not be flying with Dr Todt. The plane was to start five hours later. I was worn out and wanted only to have a decent sleep. … Next morning, the shrill clang of the telephone startled me out of a deep sleep. Dr Brant reported excitedly: "Dr Todt's plane has just crashed, and he has been killed." From that moment on my whole world was changed.'[54] **Building No. 28** was that built for Todt, which then became Speer's, and can be found behind Building No. 27. This building also houses a small hospital.[55] Opposite No. 28 is another fire water reservoir identical to Building No. 14.

Hitler held many of his meetings late at night, one of which was attended by Alexander Stahlberg, adjutant to Field Marshal Manstein. The two men were picked up by Hitler's private aircraft, flown by his personal pilot, Hans Baur, and taken to Rastenburg airfield. From there they were taken by car to the Hunters' Lodge hotel to await the summons to the *Wolfsschanze*: 'The evening briefing with Hitler generally began between 2100 and 2200. In deep darkness, we got into a train consisting of only one or two coaches, which was waiting by the guesthouse to take us in 10–15 minutes directly into the innermost restricted area of the Wolf's Lair … There was something eerie about our journey – in fact the whole of that first evening at the Führer's headquarters made an eerie impression on me. When the train stopped we got out cautiously, because here too it was pitch black. Then General Schmundt, Hitler's chief adjutant, came to welcome us. After only a few steps we arrived unexpectedly in Hitler's conference shelter, where the guests were standing grouped round the brightly-lit map table.'[56]

Speer in conversation with Hitler at the *Wolfsschanze* on 18 May 1942.

Building No. 28.

No. 28 was another two-storey building.

2

Freepost Plus RTKE-RGRJ-KTTX
Pen & Sword Books Ltd
47 Church Street
BARNSLEY
S70 2AS

A good view of the mounts supporting the steel shutters that protected the windows of all the barrack-type buildings in the *Wolfsschanze* that had not been converted into heavy concrete bunkers.

A brief mention must be made of the Hunters' Lodge, which was used as temporary accommodation for high-ranking German officers who had appointments with the Führer. It was, seemingly, comfortably appointed and a pleasant place to stay. It was surrounded by wire and protective ditches and infantry watch towers. Anyone approaching the area would see notices that read: 'No admittance to civilians. Stop. Motor Cars are not allowed to wait here longer than two minutes.' The hotel was well connected to the *Wolfsschanze*, by road and rail.

The last of our identifiable buildings in this sector, **Building No. 29**, is to the north of Speer's bunker. This was the living and working space of the liaison staff of the Reich Ministry of Defence, the *Verbindungsstab Reichsaußenminister*.

The road continues back to the visitors' car park to complete the blue route, but if instead of turning right up to the car park, one continues westwards, the buildings of *Sperrkreis* II can be found. These lay off the beaten track amid the woods to the right of the road, Here on the edge of the trees is **Building M**, the main teleprinter exchange (*nachrichtenbunker*) with its adjacent heating plant. Moving northwards is a building that illustrates the nature of the *Wolfsschanze* as a small town rather than merely a field headquarters, and this is the *kurhaus*, or spa house. This is **Building N**.

Building No. 29.

Inside No. 29.

The collapsed rear wall of No. 29.

Inside No. 29.

Building N.

The building now appears to be half-submerged.

Situated in Sperrkreis II are a number of barrack blocks of Jodl's *Wehrmachtführungsstab* (WFSt), or operational staff (**Buildings L**). Here, also is Building O, the bunker of the Commandant's Headquarters and the barracks of the FBB, **Building P**.

The *Wolfsschanze* remained occupied and fully staffed throughout the operations in the Soviet Union, ready to welcome the Führer at virtually a moment's notice. In 1944, about 2,100 people lived and worked in *Wolfsschanze*, of which about 130 were in *Sperrkreis* I. Occupying the *Wolfsschanze*, in addition to Hitler, his personal and military adjutant, orderlies, secretaries, and his cook, were Bormann, Keitel, Jodl and their respective staffs. There were detachments from the army, navy, air force and SS, the liaison offices of the Reich Chancellery and the Reich Minister Goebbels, as well as those of von Ribbentrop and Speer, along with service personnel, drivers, pilots, doctors, stenographers and, of course, the guards. The total number of troops rose from 1,277 to 1,567 officers and men.[57]

The only times this was not the case was when Hitler moved his headquarters to *Führerhauptquartiere* 'Werwolf', some 10km from Vinnytsia in Ukraine. The first of these occasions was between 16 July and 2 November 1942. During this and two subsequent periods the *Wolfsschanze* was left

Many of the buildings in *Sperrkreis* II were not converted into the massive bunkers seen in *Sperrkreis* I, allowing us to see what the buildings in the latter originally looked like.

One of the numerous barrack blocs that are found in *Sperrkreis* II.

occupied by only a minimal staff and a duty guard unit. Traudl Humps, as she was named, remained at the *Wolfsschanze* during this first occasion: 'It was strange; the hush that suddenly descended on the whole compound. It was as if the main dynamo of the concern had stopped. This was the first time I sensed how much Hitler's personality acted as a mainspring for all these men – the puppet-master, who held all the marionettes' strings in his hands, had suddenly let them fall.'

The atmosphere in the *Wolfsschanze* changed markedly as the war against the Soviet Union turned ever more decisively in favour of the Red Army. The argument that Hitler had had with Jodl that saw additional stenographers transferred to the *Wolfsschanze* also had a considerable effect on Hitler and from then on he avoided contact with his staff. He rarely went outside, only taking an occasional walk around his bunker or the nearby wood, usually at night, leaving only by the rear entrance.[58] When he did go out during the daytime he wore hats with a very large visor to shield his face from the sun.

Göring is quoted as saying in 1943 that Hitler had aged fifteen years since the start of the war: 'It is tragic that the Führer has become such a recluse and leads such an unhealthy life. He never gets out into the fresh air – he does not relax. He sits in his bunker, worries and broods. If one could only transfer him to other surroundings . . . the loneliness of general headquarters and the whole method of working there naturally have a depressing effect.'[59]

The change of mood was remarked on by Schroder: 'The festive season of 1943 passed almost unnoticed. There was no Christmas trees and no candles lit to lighten the mood.' Heinrich Hoffmann also detected a change in the mood at the *Wolfsschanze* at this time: 'The atmosphere was one of abysmal gloom, and I did my best to keep out of Hitler's way.' [60] Hoffmann turned increasingly to drink, becoming regarded as a drunkard whose ramblings caused some to think that he was becoming senile and it meant that Hitler spoke with him only rarely.

Nevertheless, work on the *Wolfsschanze* continued, with thousands of labourers working in shifts to turn the previously flimsy structures of *Sperrkreis* I into massive concrete forts. Hitler and his entourage moved out of the *Wolfsschanze* on 23 February 1944 to return to the *Berghof*, his beloved mountain retreat, while the OT teams moved in to start on the redevelopment of the site.

Over the following months the *Wolfsschanze* was extensively remodelled, with Speer spending 36 million Reichmarks reinforcing and modifying the bunkers. The place, though, was still like a building site, as Warlimont recalled: 'Hundreds of labourers were working in shifts turning the previous flimsy pillboxes of HQ Area I into mammoth concrete forts. There was a hubbub of noise and movement putting an end to the peace and security we had guarded so jealously.'[61] Though the work of strengthening the buildings was incomplete, such was the deterioration of the German position in Russia Hitler felt that he had no choice but the leave the glorious Alpine settings of Berchtesgaden for the confines of his forest headquarters, which placed him much closer to the battlefront. During the previous weeks, as Hitler enjoyed the mountain air on the Obersalzberg, the commanding generals in the East had been summoned to report to the Führer at the *Berghof*. This meant that the generals had to leave their commands for many days at a crucial point in the war. It made much more sense for Hitler to return to East Prussia.

As well as strengthening the bunkers, precautions were taken to improve the *Wolfsschanze*'s defences against aerial attack. A radar system was installed that was able to detect incoming enemy aircraft up to 60 miles away, giving several minutes' warning of an air raid. The *Führer-Luft-Nachrichten-Abteilung* (Führer Air Intelligence Detachment) had numerous observation posts to back up the radar system. If a plane was detected inside the security zone, those on an alert list of key persons were immediately evacuated to shelters by the RSD or the FBK.[62]

The *Wolfsschanze*, along with the other headquarters in the region, was integrated into the newly formed *Luftflotte Reich* (Air Fleet Reich) defence system.[63] Provision was also made to defend the *Wolfsschanze* in the event of a landing by airborne or para troops. Because of the extensive minefields and lakes that protected the area, the possibility of airborne troops risking a landing was remote. However, during the winter months the lakes froze, in which case they could provide good landing grounds. Aerial attack of some form became an increasing concern of the Führer, which he voiced in July 1944: 'The matter is so dangerous that you have to be clear ... here I sit, my entire high command sits here, the Reichsmarschall sits here, the OKH sits here, the Reichsführer SS sits here, the Reich Foreign Minister sits here! Well, that is the catch that is most worthwhile.'[64]

Hitler certainly had a point, and so anti-aircraft batteries were installed that could turn their guns on troops approaching on foot and, more particularly, could fire into the ice of the lakes, taking the ground, quite literally, from under the feet of the attackers. The number of weapons of all descriptions in the *Wolfsschanze* fluctuated over time. These were detailed by Professor Hoffman as follows:

2cm Flak 38 anti-aircraft gun	October 1941–March 1942, 22 or less; July 1942 onwards, 31.
MG 34 light machine gun	June 1941, 70; August 1941, rising to 110.
MP 38 machine pistol	June–August 1941, between 29 and 32.
3.7cm Pak 35 anti-tank gun	June–August 1941, between 17 and 21.
5cm Pak 38 anti-tank gun	June–August 1941, 2; September 1941, 13.
Heavy machine guns	May 1941–July 1942, 2 or 3.
5cm KwK 39 tank gun	May 1941–July 1942, between 7 and 9.

In September 1944, as the Red Army moved ever closer to the *Wolfsschanze*, 200 StG 44 submachine guns, 250 Luger 08 pistols, eight *Flammenwerfer* 41 flamethrowers and 500 *Raketenpanzerbüchse* 54 anti-tank rocket launchers were added to the *Wolfsschanze* armoury in addition to hand grenades, knuckledusters, lead coshes and daggers, plus an increased number of tanks and other armoured vehicles.[65]

As it transpired, the *Wolfsschanze* was not attacked before it was abandoned, and Soviet planes only dropped a few bombs on *Sperrkreis* III on a single occasion. When Soviet troops captured the *Wolfsschanze* in 1945 (see Chapter 9) a report compiled on their findings for the NVKD (People's Commissariat for Internal Affairs) observed that the site would have been 'very' difficult to penetrate.[66]

Also, in the town of Goldap, 50 miles to the north-east of the *Wolfsschanze*, a battalion of airborne troops (*Fallschirmjäger*) was stationed and held in a state of permanent readiness. From there troops could be dropped into the *Wolfsschanze* at almost a moment's notice. There were also troops stationed in barracks in Kętrzyn, Wegorzewo and Gizycko, and to the east of Kętrzyn, at Karolew, was a unit of tank destroyers.[67]

When Heinz Linge returned to the *Wolfsschanze* with Hitler and his headquarters on 9 July that year he was pleased with the improvements that had been made: 'On our return to FHQ *Wolfsschanze* we found a changed picture. The conversion work was almost complete. It looked like Ancient Egypt, the massive bunkers had a pyramid look about them. The *Führerbunker* was not yet ready, and Hitler had to move into the so-called guest's bunker which had reinforced accommodation. The situation conferences were to be held in a barrack hut with protection only against shrapnel.'[68]

That barrack hut would be the scene of the most memorable event to take place at the *Wolfsschanze*, on 20 July 1944.

Hitler's bunker now had a double-layer ceiling that was 8m thick, while the walls were about 5m thick. The foundations reached 7m down into the ground. Speer described Hitler's redesigned bunker in less than flattering terms: 'If ever a building can be considered the symbol of a situation, this bunker was it. From the outside it looked like an ancient Egyptian tomb. It was actually nothing but a great windowless block of concrete, without direct ventilation, in cross section a building whose masses of concrete far exceeded the usable cubic feet of space. It seemed as if the concrete walls sixteen and a half foot thick that surrounded Hitler separated him from the outside world

This photograph of Hitler greeting SS-Obergruppenführer Hans Gustav Gottlob Jüttner was taken in August 1944, before Hitler was able to move into his own bunker. This image may well, therefore, having been taken in the guest bunker. Himmler, Jüttner's commander, is on the right with his back to the camera.

in a figurative as well as a literal sense and locked him up inside his delusions.'[69]

Hitler's bunker depended entirely on an artificial oxygen supply when all the entrances and air intakes were closed in the event of an enemy gas attack.

Traudl Junge (*née* Humps), also returned to the *Wolfsschanze* in July 1944 with the rest of Hitler's headquarters: 'The rooms in the new bunker were small and their furnishings makeshift. Hitler set aside the hut next to it for conferences; the place had been intended for guest accommodation and had a large sitting room. Several large tables were set up here so that huge maps could be spread out, and now the place could be used as a conference room.'

With Hitler compelled to live in the guest bunker until his own was ready, *Sperrkreis* A no longer functioned as before. Instead, a new, temporary area, the Führer Restricted Zone (*Führersperrkreis*) was set up, inside which were just three buildings, with the guest bunker and the *Lagebaracke*, Building No. 3, the principal structures. The latter, as we have seen, was where the military conferences were held and where, on 20 July 1944, Claus von Stauffenberg attended his historic meeting with Hitler and many of his generals. Inside his briefcase was a bomb with a ten-minute fuse.

The *Valkyrie* assassination attempt is the subject of a separate chapter in this book, suffice it to say in this part of the guide to the *Wolfsschanze* that despite the attempt on his life, the injuries the Führer had sustained and his declining physical and, it would seem, mental health, Hitler still had a war to fight and he remained in the *Wolfsschanze*. Security was enormously increased as a consequence of the assassination attempt. Also, Hitler ordered the entrance to his bunker to be obscured by a thick concrete wall and for a machine gun nest to be formed on the roof in case his constant fear of an attack by Russian airborne troops became a reality.

He was finally able to move into his own bunker from the guest bunker in October 1944. He would not enjoy its protection for long.

Chapter 3

Oberkommando des Heeres Mauerwald

Work began on the construction of a command headquarters for the OKH – the High Command of the Army – in the autumn of 1940, approximately 11 miles to the north-east of the *Wolfsschanze*. What became known as the *Oberkommando und Generalstabes des Heeres Mauerwald* (*Mauerwald* literally means Wall Forest), also code-named 'Anna', was located on what is today the Radzieje to Węgorzewo road on elevated ground on the western shore of Lake Mamry on the south side of the Masuria Canal, at what is today Mamerki on property owned by the property of Count Lehndorff in the nearby Steinort Castle (more of whom later). It covered nearly 250 hectares and included more than 200 buildings, most of which were wooden and brick barracks, with some forty small reinforced concrete bunkers that functioned as air-raid shelters. Thirty of these bunkers and a few of the other buildings have survived to the present day. At its height some 1,500 officers, including forty or more generals, lived and worked there.

A forbidden zone extended for 5km around the installation, which consisted of a trench system and a barbed wire fence, ten watch towers, at least four guard buildings, underground shelters and anti-aircraft positions.

Before work began, the whole site was cleared, and a drainage system installed. The work was carried out by the Organisation Todt on behalf of a bogus company that had been set up in Berlin with the name Askania, the site going under the cover of 'telegraph construction site Askania'. This, it seems was a supposed branch of the Chemische Werke Askania, under which guise, as we have seen, the *Wolfsschanze* was built. During the period of construction, the workers were accommodated in barracks in nearby Wegielsztyn and Radziejów. Local labour was also employed in the form of men who had been working on the construction of the Masurian Canal. These workers were only employed at *Mauerwald* until the beginning of June 1941, when security leading up to the invasion of the Soviet Union was tightened. According to some, when work began on the expansion of *Mauerwald* in 1943, prisoners of war were used, although this remains disputed. Exact figures on the total number of men employed in the building programme are not available, but there were certainly several thousand involved – although not all at the same time. As with the *Wolfsschanze*, the workers were only kept on at *Mauerwald* for a few months before transferred elsewhere or dismissed.

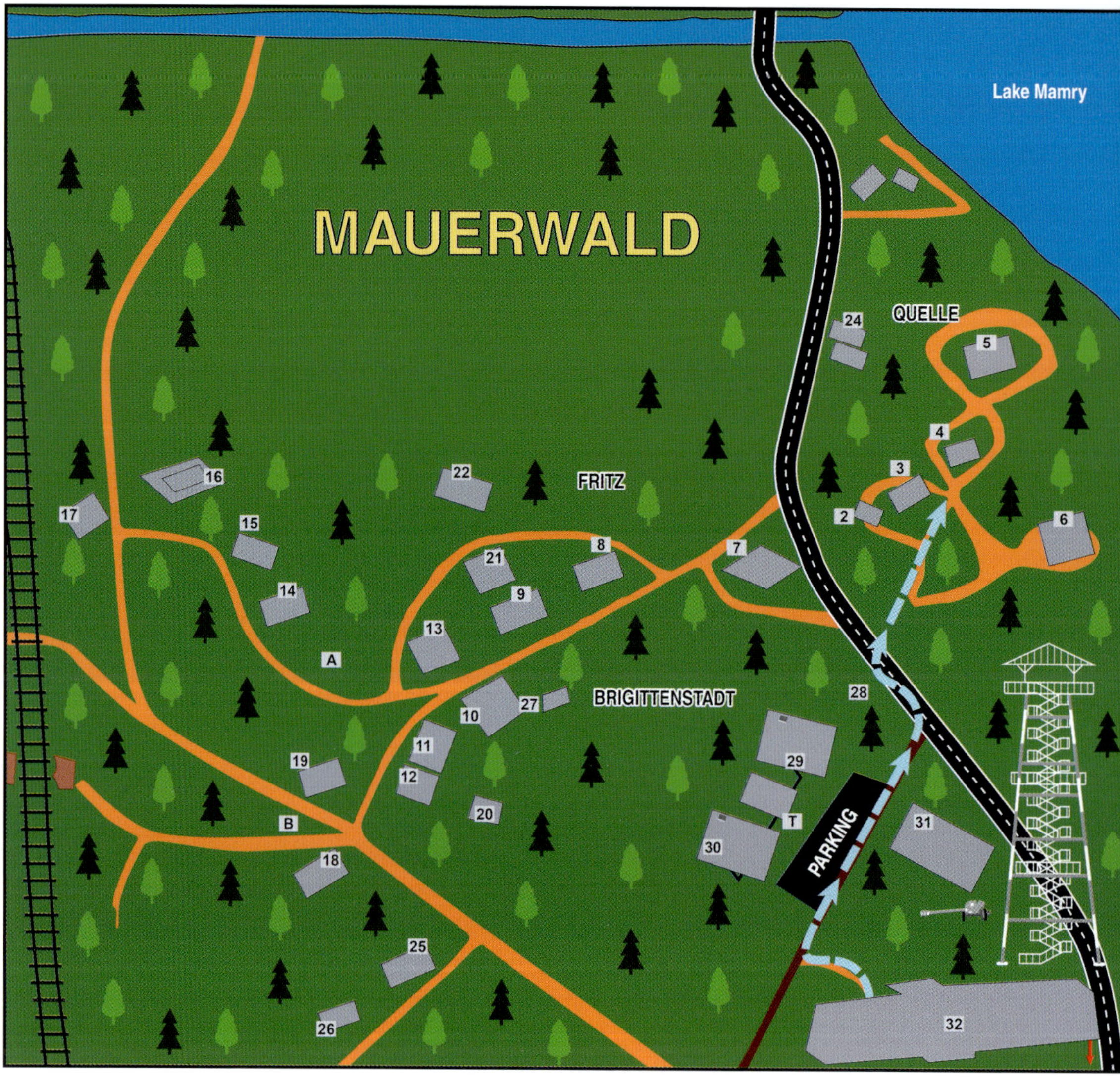

Throughout the war on the Eastern Front, *Mauerwald* operated as an independent community, with kitchens, casinos, post offices, cinemas, a hospital, a sauna and horse stables. It was surrounded on all sides with barbed wire and every 300m there were concrete pillars (still preserved today) with telephones and lanterns lighting the grounds. There were four guardhouses, and numerous anti-aircraft guns. Security generally was a little more relaxed than at the *Wolfsschanze*, with just a single mechanised battalion, a Wachbataillon of older soldiers unfit to serve in the field, responsible for its external protection, under the command of a Major Mathes. Initially two and later three companies of the Geheime Feldpolizei (Secret Field Police) guarded the installations inside.[1]

The man in charge of the entire *Mauerwald* headquarters (the Kommandeur) was Generalleutnant der Infanterie Walter von Gündel, but the day-to-day running was handled by Lagerkommandant Major Hagen, described by

Prinz von der Leyen as 'a cool and reserved Hamburger … who withstood the onslaught of wishes from above and below with irony and calm'.[2]

The *Mauerwald* complex was divided into three areas:

Zone 1 'Quelle': *Hauptquartiermeister de OKH*, the Army's quartermaster and logistics centre.

Zone 2 'Fritz': *Generalstab des OKH*, the command centre of the Army's General Staff.

Zone 3 'Brigittenstadt': *Hilfsdienst des OKH*, the main communication centre of the Army on the Eastern Front.

The following branches of the Heer were stationed at *Mauerwald*:[3]

- Central Department, which dealt with all issues related to organisation, structure and staffing of the General Staff.
- Division I Operational, which guided the whole fight in the East.
- Branch II Organisational, organisation and extension of martial law in the occupied territories.
- Branch XII (Abwehr) Foreign Armies 'East', which conducted research on the strength and intentions of the Soviet enemy and military intelligence materials.
- Military Attaché Department, which managed the activity of German military attachés abroad. In the OKH headquarters there were military attaches from Finland (Lieutenant General Paavo Talvela), Hungary (General József Vasváry) and the Japanese Lieutenant General Ichiryō Banzai.
- Personnel Management OKH, which dealt with staffing of military commanders on the front.

There were more than fifty buildings in 'Quelle', most of which were wooden barracks set on brick foundations. They were built in large numbers on behalf of the OKH as general-purpose buildings. Air-raid protection for personnel in these buildings was offered by the bunkers.

Depending on the type, the bunkers at *Mauerwald* had two or five rooms and two or four loopholes locked from the inside. The bunkers were fully supplied with electricity, and equipped with ventilation systems, telephones, central heating and toilets. The entrances of the bunkers had gas-tight reinforced doors. As with the improvements at the *Wolfsschanze*, the *Mauerwald* bunkers were upgraded with a huge concrete shell, built on a 17.5m × 21.5m foundation that was 3.5m thick. The roofs had a 40cm 'basin' into which soil was placed and trees and shrubs planted.

Prinz Ferdinand von der Leyden was on the staff of the General Quartermaster in the OKH: 'The first days in "Quelle", as our camp district was called, memories are a bit lost. Too many new things, too many new people, who only gradually took shape and face, too many new impressions stormed me. First the local problem: the darkness under the trees became as good as impenetrable. Finding a desired barracks (there was no one who knew their way around) was a feat. All living and working accommodations were scattered around the forest in a completely random manner, only following the requirement of visibility from above. Not even house-to-house paths, as they later emerged, gave any clue. In addition, the number of the individual departments could not be overlooked, at least for a newcomer to the High Command of the Army like me.'[4]

The intake from Lake Mamry delivered water to the pumping station and water treatment plant. Electricity was supplied from the grid to transformer stations, and diesel generators placed in generating stations provided power in case of failure from the grid. Boiler rooms supplied buildings with heat.

As with the *Wolfsschanze*, measures were taking to mask the buildings from the air. Covering exterior walls with seagrass hardened with concrete and with a special moss have effectively protected the bunkers from exposing their position so that even now, after seventy years, the bunkers merge with the forest. OKH *Mauerwald* was integrated into the air defence system of Air Fleet Reich, as was the *Wolfsschanze* and the other headquarters installations in the area. This had an effective radar coverage of 150km. The Luftwaffe's Air Intelligence department also set up a chain of observation posts.

On 21 May 1941, the Generalstab moved to *Mauerwald*, with Generaloberst Franz Halder arriving at Zone 2 on 23 June 1941. The Commander-in-Chief of the Heer, Generalfeldmarschall Walter von Brauchitsch, arrived for the first time on 25 June, joining Halder in 'Fritz'.

Brauchitsch's staff found *Mauerwald* ready for immediate use, with a fully functional communications network to all army groups and armies deployed against the Soviet Union. In the previous seven months, a total of 1,366km of trunk and aerial cables had been designed and installed by the Deutsche Reichspost. Just before the beginning of *Barbarossa* more than 600 telephone lines had been made available to senior staff, along with telegraph lines.[5]

As mentioned previously, the OKH headquarters had a railroad connection to the *Wolfsschanze* and to Himmler's *Schwarzschanze*, as well as to the quarters of the head of the Reich Chancellery Hans-Heinrich Lammers, which was in the forest next to Rosengarten. A train ran each day from *Mauerwald* to the *Wolfsschanze* to take the officers of the General Staff to attend Hitler's situation conferences.

The daily routine of the Operations Department at *Mauerwald* began at 08.30 hours with the receipt of the morning reports from the front, including the movements of the enemy. This was followed at 09.30 with the issuing of instructions for the work of the day. At 10.15 there was a 'lecture' on the current situation to the Chief of the General Staff to the Army, which was then presented to the Commander-in-Chief of the Army (this was only until 19 December 1941, when Hitler took over command of the Army).

Staff of the *Operationsabteilung des OKH*, or Operations Department of the Army at *Mauerwald* in September 1943.

From 12.30 hours until 15.00 hours, or longer, the Chief of the General Staff had to brief Hitler on the current war situation. This, usually, meant a trip over to the *Wolfsschanze*.

At 16.00 hours there was a meeting of the heads of the various operations groups followed by a report to the Wehrmacht High Command and other Wehrmacht units. At 17.00 hours, telephone discussions were held with other department heads of the Army General Staff.

Interim reports on the day's operations were received from the various army groups at 19.30 hours, and at 21.00 hours there was a further lecture to the Chief of the General Staff. An hour later that individual had to brief the Commander-in-Chief, this, again, normally being at the *Wolfsschanze*. Whatever instructions were forthcoming from the evening briefing were then issued to the various army groups. Finally, between 01.00 and 03.00 hours was the final receipt of the end-of-day report from the army groups.

In the early days at *Mauerwald*, when Operation *Barbarossa* appeared to be succeeding, the atmosphere was light-hearted, as one of Generalfeldmarschall Erich von Manstein's orderlies, Alexander Stahlberg, recalled on a visit to the OKH on 13 July 1941. Manstein's party arrived in the afternoon only to learn that the conference they were due to attend was not scheduled until the evening. What, the men asked each other, were they going to do for eight hours? 'We will go for a swim,' the generalfeldmarschall suggested. Stahlberg was not too happy at this, as the men had not come prepared for

Hitler and Mussolini visiting *Mauerwald* during the Italian leader's August 1941 trip to the *Wolfsschanze* in those happier early days.

such an experience. Manstein told his orderly not to worry, there were no civilians allowed in the area of the complex. 'We will get undressed in our rooms, and then cover ourselves with our cloaks'.

The men undressed and slipped out of the guesthouse, 'and came across a wide wooden pier cutting into the strip of the reeds of Lake Mamry. Along the way, we did not meet anyone, and shortly – just as God created us – we pushed to the centre of the lake. Only one who knows the beauty of Masuria can know how we felt at that time. Around the water and forests, not one village, not a single house!' They had swum 200–300 metres away from the pier when they saw a group of men by the shore – amongst whom was Generalleutnant Erwin Rommel! The military paths of the two generals had not crossed before, but Rommel bellowed out a thunderous 'Hello', to which Manstein replied, 'We meet at last!'

Manstein's men hauled themselves out of the water, only to find that their cloaks had disappeared. They stood there completely naked in front of Rommel, who, pretending not to notice their embarrassment, introduced his officers to them! Eventually Rommel ordered his men to hand over the cloaks.

The mood changed considerably after Hitler assumed command of the armed forces on 19 December 1941. But there was one last memorable experience recorded by Prinz Leyden on 25 December of that first year at

Mauerwald. 'The harsh winter in the East Prussian forest was a wonderful background for Christmas. The Chief of the General Staff, Halder, invited us all to celebrate the evening in the open air. In the clearing stood a huge fir tree, radiantly lit upwards by electric candles. The Christmas tree could not have looked more beautiful in the trembling, creaking forest.'

Hitler visited *Mauerwald* on just three occasions. The first was to celebrate General Halder's birthday, on 30 June 1941, and the second time was in August 1941, when he took Mussolini there to see the complex. So secure did Hitler consider himself to be at that stage of the war that the two leaders travelled by the normal car that shuttled constantly between the *Wolfsschanze* and *Mauerwald*.

Hitler's last visit was on 14 July 1942, which marked Halder's forty years of military service. Hitler gave Halder a signed silver-framed portrait of himself. Other notable visitors included the Hungarian dictator Miklos Horty, the Romanian head of state Jon Antonescu, and the commander-in-chief of the Finnish armed forces, Baron Carl Gustaf Emil Mannerheim.

Such was the scale of the operations against the Soviet Union, *Mauerwald* quickly grew to become the largest bunker complex built by the Germans. According to Prinz van der Leyen, the site was so vast that even after a year

Hitler discusses the military situation with von Brauchitsch (first from the left) and Halder, Chief of the General Staff of the Land Forces (right), at *Mauerwald* during his visit in August 1941.

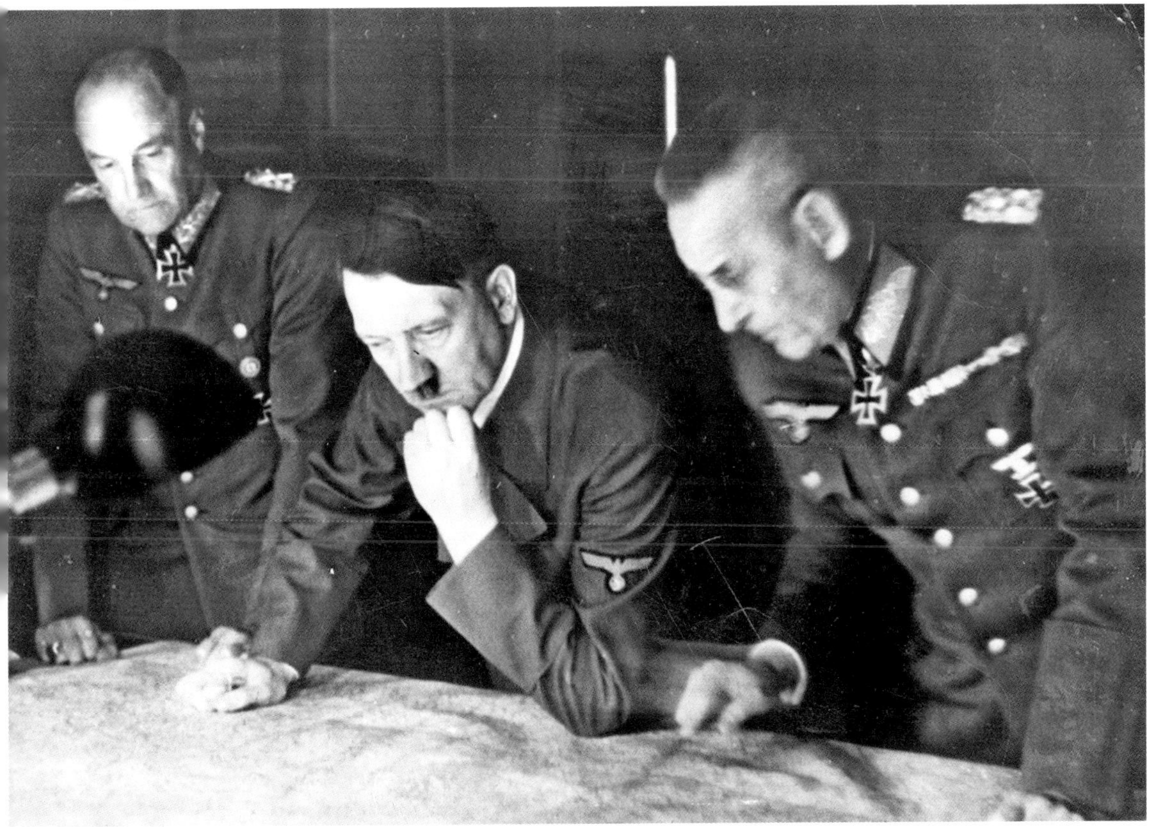

Hitler visited *Mauerwald* a second time in October 1941. From the right: Wilhelm Keitel, Adolf Hitler, Walther von Brauchitsch and Friedrich Paulus.

many of the staff still did not know the names of individual branches and offices.

The food on offer for the staff at *Mauerwald* was, according to von der Leyden modest, simple but sufficient. Alcohol was carefully rationed through a voucher system to ensure moderate drinking, with vouchers being given out monthly. Officers arriving at *Mauerwald* from the front were usually given better fare in the dining room.

An unspoken rule among the staff at *Mauerwald* was that politics or economics would never be discussed: 'The political ignorance of the officers was appalling,' declared von der Leyen. 'Most of them preferred not to know too much. Their average attitude is "Thank God, we are not dealing with these matters." One evening, when Berlin-based Oberst Claus von Stauffenberg was in the dining room, he broke the rule. His explanation of the dire situation Germany was in created what von der Leyen called: 'The darkest evening I have ever spent in camp.'

As with the *Wolfsschanze*, OKH *Mauerwald* was significantly strengthened during the course of the war. There were three phases in its development. Initially, with the campaign against the Soviet Union expected to be of a short duration, only light bunkers and wooded barrack blocks were built – even the Chief of the General Staff initially worked in a normal wooden barracks. The large bunkers that can be seen today, as with those at the *Wolfsschanze*, came in the third building phase in 1944. The strength of their construction can be gauged by the fact that while they weigh as much as an estimated 15,000 tons, more than seventy years later none have collapsed under their weight or sunk in the inherently marshy and swampy ground. As with the large *Wolfsschanze* bunkers, these *Mauerwald* bunkers had metal rung ladders running up the outside walls to reach the roofs. The wooden buildings, particularly those in the 'Brigittenstadt' section, no longer exist.

Living conditions at *Mauerwald* were regarded as being far more pleasant, and healthier, than the *Wolfsschanze* trapped in its gloomy, insect-infested, swampy forest, though today the mosquitoes have found their way to *Mauerwald* and are every bit as voracious as their *Wolfsschanze* cousins.

This favourable view of *Mauerwald* was certainly one entertained by Prinz Ferdinand von der Leyen, who described his arrival there from Berlin: 'Our transport train rolled east, from which, as expected, East Prussia gradually became recognisable as the destination. In the middle of the next morning, the train, on what appeared to be an open stretch of track, stopped next to a forest in the vicinity of Angerburg: we had arrived. Only a small loading ramp seemed to indicate that there was no mistake. We were led into a splendid,

Mauerwald's lovely setting close to Lake Mamry. The structure below is Building No. 32.

mixed forest, in which ancient oaks prevailed. More and more wooden barracks and a few chunky concrete bunkers became visible in the deep shadows of the trees.'

He saw: 'More and more wooden barracks and occasional massive, concrete presidential bunkers in the forest cover. All living quarters and work rooms were irregularly dispersed in the forest. The art was to find a barrack or accommodation block, especially in the dark. Our camp was bordered by one side with the wonderful Lake Mamry, the shores of which could be glimpsed through the walls of the magnificent tree surrounds, making the settlement seem more human.'

When Prinz Ferdinand first arrived at *Mauerwald* at the start of the campaign against the Soviet Union, he wrote in his memoirs that he thought that the bunkers and barracks had to be built quickly to accommodate the large influx of personnel that would inevitably occur. This is indeed exactly what happened, and he later wrote that: 'I watched the camp spread very quickly. The number of arriving offices was infinite, countless.'

As can be seen in this aerial photograph, the density of the tree cover at *Mauerwald* was also far from complete, especially in autumn (when this photograph was taken) and winter, when many of the trees had shed their leaves.

Prinz Ferdinand spent several years at *Mauerwald* working in the Quartermaster General's department and left a memoir of his time at the OKH: 'The General Quartermaster was responsible for the proper supply of the land forces alongside many others. From ammunition and gasoline to the mail and cigarettes, from all medical needs to horses, everything you can think of ... The further the war expanded, the difficulties became greater ... The provision of transport for every military action became a bigger problem. Transportation lengthened from 120km to 600km and even further.'[6]

Visitors today arrive at the coach and car park opposite the entrance to Zone I 'Quelle'. As with the *Wolfsschanze*, there are three tours visitors can take. The red route, which tours round the main buildings in 'Quelle', is 600m in length. The 1km red route is around the main structures of 'Brigittenstadt', excluding Building No. 32, and the yellow route of 2.5km runs around much of 'Fritz'. All visitors will want to add the 'Giant' Bunker (Building No. 32), to their itinerary.

The first, very large bunker on the right in 'Quelle' (**Building No. 6**) was for Division III Foreign Armies West (*Fremde Heere West*), which was responsible for gathering and interpreting information on the plans and intentions of Germany's enemies in Western Europe, the UK and the United States. There is an entrance to the shelter and internal rooms from the corridor. The bunker also served as a shelter in the event of an air attack for all intelligence staff, with double reinforced concrete walls, 6m thick. Some hooks or staples that held the camouflage netting are still present on the outside of the bunker. Next to this bunker are the foundations of long-gone brick barracks and the office of the head of Department III, Lieutenant Colonel Ulrich Liss.

Opposite Building No. 6 is **Building No. 2**, which was a typical Type B bunker, with walls just 2m thick. It has just two rooms but is of interest in that it has well-preserved loopholes for defence.

To its right is another Type B bunker (**Building No. 4**), which in this instance has five small rooms, and beyond that, the huge bunker of General der Artillerie Eduard Wagner's department, **Building No. 5**. Wagner was the Quartermaster-General of the German Army (*Generalquartiermeister im Oberkommando des Heeres*) and next to this bunker are the remains of his quarters, **Building B**. This 20m × 8m house had a terrace with a view of the lake. The foundations can still be seen, as well as the remains of a fireplace. There was also a basement in which there was a sauna, where the 20 July 1944 conspirators met to discuss their plans to assassinate Hitler. They met there because the sound of water drowned out the conversation.

Original information details are disappearing through the ravages of time and weather and disappointingly disfigured by graffiti.

There are the foundations of numerous other buildings in 'Quelle', including a canteen just to the east of the parking area, behind which was another sauna, and three guard posts, or 'Wachposten'.

Building No. 6.

A far better impression of what it must have been like inside the bunkers can be gained from those at *Mauerwald* than at the *Wolfsschanze*.

Numerous fixtures and fittings are still in place in the bunkers.

Defensive loopholes can be found in many of the bunkers.

The huge steel hinges give some indication of just how heavy the doors of the bunkers were.

As was the case at the *Wolfsschanze*, and as can be seen here, access to the flat roofs of the buildings was possible via exterior metal steps.

Building No. 2.

This photograph gives some indication of the scale and complexity of the telecommunications network which served *Mauerwald*.

The entrance to Building No. 2.

The narrow corridors in Building No. 2 are repeated in the other bunkers.

More of the original electrical fittings can still be seen.

Adjacent to this is **Building No. 3**, which was a transformer station.

There are a number of information boards around the site, such as this in Building No. 3.

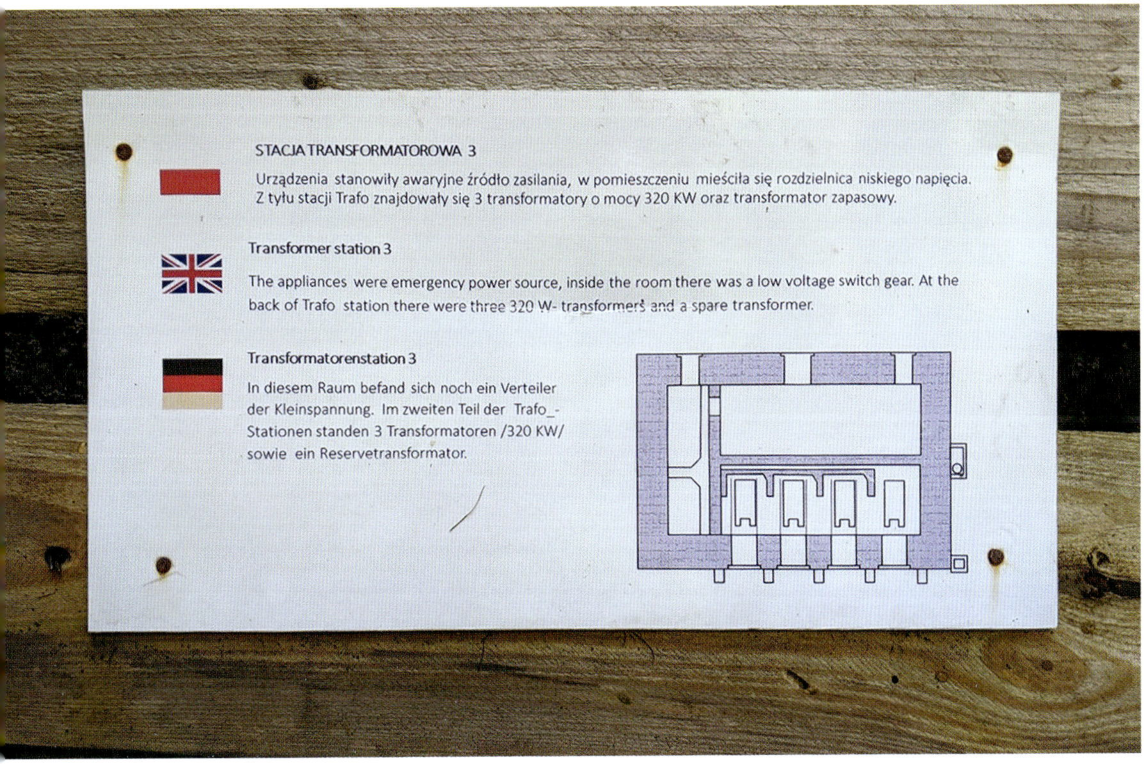

Inside the transformer station 3.

Building No. 4.

Again, another almost perfectly preserved fitting can be seen on the outside of defence bunker No. 4.

Building No. 5.

The green dye with which the camouflage was coloured is still visible on many of the bunkers, such as here on Building No. 5.

Original information details disappearing through the ravages of time and weather and disappointingly disfigured by graffiti.

According to this information board, Hitler, the erstwhile artist, drew the plan for No. 4.

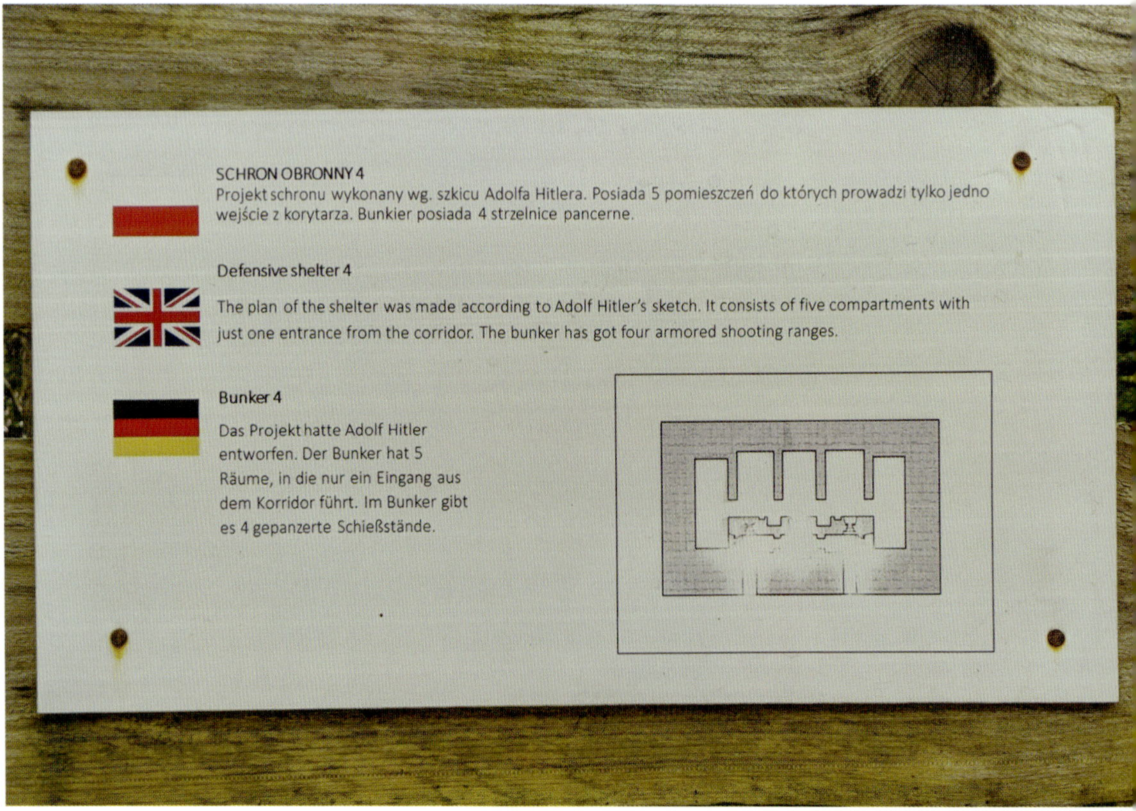

Returning towards the parking lot, and continuing south along the road, the visitor can walk along a pathway to Zone III 'Brigittenstadt'. Here are large interconnected bunkers (**Buildings 20**, **29** and **30**) which housed a command and communication centre, and provided a usable space of more than 600 sq m. They are linked by a 30m passage, or tunnel, and the rooms now house a small museum.

On the opposite side of the parking area is the location of **Building No. 31**. This is the foundations of a huge building, but there are differing opinions regarding its intended use. Whereas one map of *Mauerwald* refers to it being an air-raid shelter, another describes it as being the foundations of a new communications centre. More recently it has been suggested that it is a subterranean bunker that houses the long-lost Amber Room – more of which shortly. Indeed, geo-radar has shown that there is a tunnel under the structure and a hatch above it has been discovered. At the time of writing, permission is being sought from the Polish authorities to open the hatch.

The steel roof supports still look solid.

Building No. 29.

Part of the interconnecting passageways.

Unlike other buildings, these three linked buildings have quite spacious rooms.

The interconnecting subterranean tunnel.

Building No. 30.

The main pathways through *Mauerwald* are surfaced in the same manner as those at the *Wolfsschanze*.

Building No. 31.

The approach to No. 31.

Beyond this enigmatic structure, a path leads southwards to the large bunker, **Building No. 32**. As *Mauerwald* has become a tourist attraction, there are exhibition rooms in this bunker which give details of some of the Third Reich's more ambitious projects. This includes the so-called 'bell' (*Die Glocke*), which was supposedly an anti-gravity device, as well as the entirely genuine Horten Ho 229 'flying wing', the forerunner of the stealth aircraft of today, the Haunebu III flying disk, and the V2 rocket. Of further interest is a diorama of the Siege of Stalingrad, a small collection of German and Soviet uniforms and a reproduction of the famous Amber Room. This dazzling room was decorated in amber panels (more than 6 tons of amber was used in its construction) backed with gold leaf and mirrors. It was originally built in Prussia in the eighteenth century but was given by the Prussian king to Peter the Great of Russia and was installed in the Catherine Palace outside St Petersburg (later Leningrad). During the Siege of Leningrad, the Amber Room was dismantled by Army Group North and taken to Königsberg, but then, seemingly, it disappeared – possibly being hidden at *Mauerwald*. If the excavation mentioned above proceeds, the answer may be found to one of the Second World War's most puzzling mysteries.

An aerial view of the large bunker, Building No. 32.

There is also a 25m-long model of a German U-boat, which visitors can enter, and a tall observation tower can be climbed with views over Lake Mamry. The tower also provides a bird's-eye view of the *Mauerwald* site, which shows just how well concealed the entire complex was from the air.

To investigate Zone II 'Fritz', it is advisable to walk back to the parking lot. From there you will find **Building No. 7**, a water treatment and pumping station.

Walking beyond No. 7, and turning left down the road, the visitor arrives at a cluster of bunkers. These are **Building No. 8**, which is another two-roomed Type 'B' bunker, as is **Building No. 9** and **Building No. 21**, which is set to the west behind Nos 8 and 9.

The next one along the road on this same side is **Building No. 13**, which was the accommodation for the head of the Fremde Heere Ost (FHO), Generalleutnant Reinhard Gehlen. Like its counterpart, Fremde Heere West, Gehlen's department focussed on gathering intelligence against Germany's enemies, in this case the Soviet Union. From 1942, Fremde Heere Ost also had a base at Fortress Boyen, which is briefly examined later in this book.

The road branches at this point. Taking the left-hand fork, on the left side of the road is, **Building No. 27** another two-room bunker. Next to this is **Building No. 10**, which was a transformer station.

Building No. 7.

The entrance to Building No. 7 is now partially submerged.

The severely ruined interior of No. 7.

Building No. 8.

Inside Building No. 8.

Building No. 10.

Inside Building No. 10.

Building No. 11 was a central heating boiler room and, next to this, is **Building No. 12**, which was the power plant for No. 11. The internal dimensions of No. 11 and No. 12, at 21m × 13m, are so large that when the site was investigated after the war, it was thought that these were factory buildings that were to be used for the assembly of U-boats, which, when completed, were to be sailed through the Masurian Canal down to the Baltic. This created a legend that still endures despite being disproven.

In order to see some of the other major buildings in 'Fritz', it is necessary to return along the road to where it divided, this time taking what is now the left-hand fork. Here, on the right, the foundations of **Building A** can be seen. This was the quarters of the Army Chief of Staff, the Chef des Generalstabs des Heeres. Throughout the course of the war in the East, this post was held by a number of different officers. The first of these was Generaloberst Franz Halder, who held the post until 24 September 1942. General der Infanterie Kurt Zeitzler served until 1 July 1944, being replaced by Generalleutnant Adolf Heusinger, who was stood next to Hitler when von Stauffenberg's bomb exploded on 20 July 1944. He was replaced the day after the assassination attempt by Generaloberst Heinz Guderian, who was the last Chief of Staff to occupy this building.

Building No. 11.

Inside Building No. 11.

Building No. 12.

Inside the power plant No. 12.

Another view inside No. 12.

The next bunker on the right is **Building No. 14**. This bunker was used by Adolf Heusinger as head of the *Operationsabteilung*, or Operations Department of the Army. When he became Chief of Staff, he also retained his *Operationsabteilung* post. In the spring of 1942 Wolf-Dietrich Freiherr von Schenk zu Tautenburg joined Heusinger's *Operationsabteilung* at *Mauerwald*. For each Army Group in the field there was a corresponding working group in the Operations Department. Each working group was usually headed by a lieutenant colonel, with two staff officers with the rank of major or captain and two lieutenants. Tautenburg was part of the working group responsible to Army Group South: 'The work ... started in the morning at 10.00 hours and ended at 10.00 the next day. During the course of the day, events on the front were entered on a 1:300,000 scale map. In the evening around 19.00 hours a meeting took place with General Heusinger. From 20.00 hours, or later, the total results of the day were received from the army group, and the exact front line had to be drawn on the map. The following day at around 09.30 hours, there would be another presentation of the situation to General Heusinger,' and the daily routine would begin again.[7]

Building No. 15 was that used by General der Nachrichtentruppe, Fritz Erich Fellgiebel, who was Chief Signal Officer of Army High Command and of Supreme Command of Armed Forces. As head of communications, Fellgiebel had a key role in the *Valkyrie* assassination attempt. His involvement, more of which later, was obvious and he was arrested, sentenced to death and executed.

Building No. 15.

Also on the right side of the road is **Building No. 16** used by General der Infanterie Rudolf Gercke, who was the OKH's head of transportation, or Chef des Feldtransportwesens.

Just after Building No. 16, the road reached a junction. This is where **Building No. 17**, the ruins of the railway station, is located. Just to the west of the station building is the railway line that, it may be recalled, connected all the headquarters sites associated with the *Wolfsschanze*.

Walking southwards from the railway station, **Building No. 19** on the right-hand side of the road was for the Kriegsmarine liaison department, under Kommandant Heinrich-Dietrich Conradi. Just beyond this building the road is joined by a track road from the right. By following this track **Building No. 18** can be found. This two-room bunker was for the Chef der Organisationsabteilung (Coordination Department) Generalmajor Hellmuth Stieff, under the command of Heusinger. Like his boss, he was involved in the assassination attempt of 20 July and he too was arrested and executed.

Returning to the road, and continuing southwards, **Building No. 20** on the left is a two-room bunker. After a few more metres along the road, another track joins it from the right. Along this track can be found **Building No. 25** and **Building No. 26**, which are both two-room bunkers. This completes the number of surviving bunkers in 'Fritz'.

Building No. 16.

No.16 is heavily overgrown.

Building No. 17.

Scant remains beside the railway track which joined *Mauerwald* to the *Wolfsschanze*.

Mauerwald was in constant use by the OKH during the war in the Soviet Union apart from a short period from 16 July until 2 November 1942 when, along with all the other headquarters in the region, the OKH transferred to Vinnytsia in Ukraine. Though Hitler stayed at his *Führerhauptquartier Werwolf* just outside Vinnytsia (investigated further in this book), the OKH staff were quartered in the city itself during that time.

The main function of OKH *Mauerwald* was to direct the Heer's war effort against the Soviets, and in 1943, its already vast telecommunications system was supplemented by newly developed radio communications links operated by dedicated units. However, in July 1944, Generaloberst Heinz Guderian was promoted to Chief of the General Staff of the Army and he took up his position at *Mauerwald*, coincidentally, on the fateful 20th of that month, but found that communications were not exactly as he expected: 'I went to Mamerek, to the barracks where the offices of the head of the General Staff were located – my new workplace. The barracks was empty. Nobody was waiting to greet me. I searched all the rooms and only in the last room I found a sleeping soldier named Riehl. I sent this man to get an officer . . . Then I tried to make contact with the staffs of army groups to get an idea of the situation on the front. I gave my name, shouted and hung up the phone. It was a long time before I was able to calm down and put the phone down, . . . and it took a long time before I was able to make contact [with the group commanders].'

Building No. 25.

Chapter 4

Feldkommandostelle Hochwald

Map Coordinates: 54°08′59.6″N 21°51′12.2″E; 54.14984, 21.853395

As with the Heer, the SS had its own headquarters complex in East Prussia. Work on what was called *Hochwald* (High forest) was completed in the spring of 1941 some 16 miles to the east of the *Wolfsschanze* near the village of what was Großgarten and is today's Pozezdrze. The complex was just next to the Kętrzyn–Węgorzewo–Giżycko railway line, with its own siding with a platform for Himmler's train, the Sonderzug *Heinrich*. The railway facilitated communication and served to deliver a huge amount of materials needed for the construction. The railway carriages of Foreign Minister Ribbentrop and head of the Reich Chancellery Hans Lammers, who had their own headquarters in the region, were also kept in this siding. When the Red Army

Himmler on one of his visits to East Prussia shown here with Hitler congratulating him on his 43rd birthday at the *Wolfsschanze* on 7 October 1943.

discovered the site in 1944 they found that where the trains were stationed was so well camouflaged that they would have been difficult to spot, even at close distance. The siding was heavily protected by both barbed wire and infantry positions. *Hochwald* soon acquired the nickname *Schwarzschanze* (*schwarz* means 'black') because of the black parade uniforms of the SS.

A number of well-camouflaged bunkers and barracks were constructed on the 4 sq km site and, as with the other headquarters, *Hochwald* was heavily protected with wire mesh fence, barbed wire, minefields and high watch towers set up in trees. There were also defensive infantry positions and the site was heavily guarded by a battalion of police.[1] Just like the *Wolfsschanze*, signs warned civilians not to deviate from the approach road.

There were five concrete bunkers, a small underground garage, two brick guardhouses and an extra-large bunker for Himmler. One of the buildings was a small prison with concrete cells which was guarded by a special police battalion commanded by a Sturmbannführer Krumme.[2] When this field command post became too small, twenty wooden barracks were built scattered around the forest for the staff of forty-eight people.

Himmler's bunker.

Himmler avoided *Hochwald* as much as possible and it is understood that when there he spent most of his time in his train, which had its own cinema, rather than here in his bunker. He also commandeered a local house, which in his service diary he either called Friedrichsruh or it was at a location of that name.

Inside Himmler's bunker.

Although overgrown, the remains at *Hochwald* are accessible.

The external dimensions of the standard bunkers were 13.7m × 10.7m, each with a double entrance 80cm wide. To enter a bunker, a visitor had to pass through the outer armoured door into a lock. Only when this door was closed behind the visitor would the inner armoured door be opened. The interior of the bunkers was filled with two work rooms equipped with their own lighting and ventilation system. The concrete on the walls and roof was 2m thick.

Himmler's huge bunker measured 70m × 11m wide. As with some of the other bunkers in the *Wolfsschanze*, Himmler's bunker was strengthened in 1944, the concrete shell being doubled in thickness. Unlike the *Wolfsschanze*, however, no anti-aircraft guns or machine guns were placed in or on the bunkers.

Hochwald can be found today by following the road from Pozezdrze to Gizycko. Just outside Pozezdrze on the right-hand side of the road is a small white signpost with blue lettering, which reads 'Kwatera Bunkera Himmlera' with a simple outline of a bunker. The turnoff leads to a neglected car park, from where a path leads through the trees and undergrowth to the complex. The most complete of the buildings is Himmler's large bunker.

For two weeks in November 1942, SS headquarters was moved temporarily to Kruglanken, today's Kruklanki, approximately 4½ miles to the south.

Himmler's bunker from above. This photograph shows the way in which the flat roofs of the bunkers across all the East Prussian headquarters sites were laid out with grass to conceal them from above. *(Mariusz Switulski/Shutterstock)*

The access road to *Hochwald*.

As with the other sites, nature is slowly embracing *Hochwald*.

The *Feldkommandostelle* operated functionally during the attack on the Soviet Union on 22 June 1941. For two weeks in November 1942, the HQ was moved temporarily to Kruglanken, about 4 or 5 miles to the south.[3] As the war moved deep into Russia, a new SS headquarters – *Hegewald* – was established some 900km to the south-east.

The *Hochwald* was destroyed by German sappers on 24 January 1945.

Chapter 5

Oberkommando der Luftwaffe, Robinson

As with the Heer, the Luftwaffe established its headquarters for the campaign in Eastern Europe near the *Wolfsschanze*. As it happened, Hermann Göring and his staff were already frequent visitors to the area. From 1936, they had often visited the Romincka Forest on hunting trips, staying at a manor house, the Jägerhof Rominten (also known as the Reichsjägerhof). In 1938 the forest was given the status of a state hunting district. In 1940 an air-raid shelter was built next to the manor for Göring and his staff.

The Luftwaffe had its headquarters in East Prussia for the invasion of the Soviet Union in the town of Breitenheide, today's Szeroki Bór. However, due to design errors, as well as the need for its staff to be close to Göring, the headquarters were moved to Kumiecie Forest, near Lake Goldap, very close to the Russian border, and more than 50 miles from the *Wolfsschanze*.

Göring, however, preferred to monitor Luftwaffe operations from his lavishly appointed personal armoured train, *Pommern* (also known as *Asien*). His command staff also had their own train, *Robinson*, and when their command post was built in East Prussia close to Göring's residence, it was named after this train.

Compared with the *Wolfsschanze* and *Mauerwald*, the *Robinson* site was small, consisting of just one heavily fortified bunker for Göring and his staff, two personnel barracks, six brick buildings and three large fire tanks. It was built amid the trees of the forest, with concealment an obvious factor. The site was defended by Regiment 'Hermann Göring'.

The first summer at *Robinson* was a difficult one for the Reichsmarschall. The humid climate affected him badly and he received almost daily check-ups by his cardiologist, Professor Heinrich Zahler.[1]

Always mindful of the possible need to change locations at a moment's notice, Göring's two special trains, hidden under camouflage nets, were kept at nearby stations in a state of readiness – *Robinson* at Schakummen in Eichkamp, which was built specifically for the Luftwaffe train, and, until 1 February 1943, *Pommern* at Gross Kummetschen. Göring's personal train consisted of eight coaches, which included two saloon cars equipped with a library and desks and a bath/hairdressing coach.[2]

The sole large bunker in *Robinson*.

For added protection, the entrance was set below ground level.

As with the *Wolfsschanze*, *Robinson* was demolished by the Germans ahead of the advancing Red Army. The order for this was issued on 1 June 1944 and was carried out on the night of 19/20 October 1944 under the code name *Johannisfeuer*.

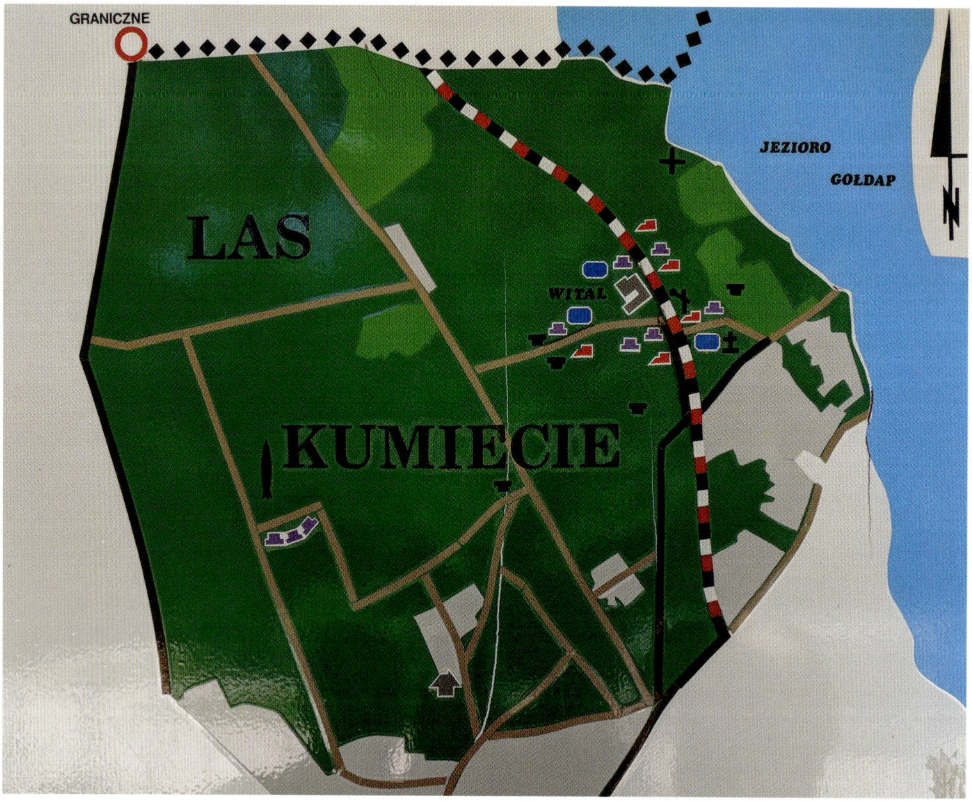

A rudimentary plan of *Robinson* is displayed at the site. The blue rectangles are swimming pools, the red ones are 'ruins and foundation of the buildings', and the T-shaped buildings are somewhat enigmatically referred to as 'Airshow boxes'.

A machine gun loophole can be seen on the far wall of the large bunker.

A close-up of the machine gun loophole seen opposite.

A photograph of Göring at one of the East Prussian headquarters, but it is not possible to specify whether this is at *Robinson* or the *Wolfsschanze*.

All that remains of some of the brick-build buildings are their foundations.

Protection was clearly a key consideration during the building of *Robinson* with shielded entrances to some of the buildings.

Some of the remains at *Hochwald* are difficult to identify.

The walls inside the bunkers were plastered.

The entrance to this building is interesting in that the entrance opening was shielded from direct fire by the wall seen here on the left of the photograph. This can perhaps be better seen in the following two photographs.

These smaller buildings were also loopholed for defence.

What appears to be a fire water reservoir similar to those at the *Wolfsschanze*.

A guard post on one of the approach roads to *Robinson*.

A research facility for the engines of the V2 rocket was also housed in the Kumiecie Forest around 1.5km from *Robinson*. It was constructed in either 1939 or 1940. This consisted of a dozen or so buildings and forty somewhat enigmatic pillars in a small gorge. There was an observation shelter in the gorge that was reportedly intact until the 1980s. The building included three

One of the numerous pillars in the V2 testing facility.

The remnants of the V-2 testing facility.

light shelters buried in the ground, and several technical shelters, guard-houses and other structures. There are no restrictions to access either the *Robinson* or V2 sites.

In the 1970s, part of the *Robinson* complex believed to have functioned as the Luftwaffe dining rooms were adapted to the canteen and cafe of the RTV centre, currently the 'Wital' sanatorium at Wczasowa 7, 19-500 Gołdap.

The friendly staff at the gate are happy to allow visitors to park in the sanatorium's car park if the purpose of your visit is explained to them. There are no restrictions and the site can be walked freely.

Chapter 6

Other Headquarters in East Prussia

Hauptquartier des Chef der Reichskanzlei

SS-Obergruppenführer Hans-Heinrich Lammers, head of the Reich Chancellery (*Reichskanzleichef*), had his own small bunker complex, which he named 'Wendula', near the village of Rosengarten, which is today's Polish town of Radzieje. It was well situated, being a little more than 6 miles from the *Wolfsschanze* to the south-west and 3 miles from *Mauerwald* in the opposite direction.

Wendula can be found by following the Węgorzewska road northwards through Radzieje – the main road through the town – for approximately 2.2km to an unnamed straight road on the left that runs at right angles to the Węgorzewska road. This road runs towards the forest for just under a

Hans Lammers, standing next to Himmler, at an address to members of the East Prussian *Volkssturm* battalions, the first *Volkssturm* to take up arms, in late October 1944.

kilometre, where it bends sharply to the left. At this point a path leads to the right towards Wendula. Its decimalised map coordinates are 54.148482, 21.593018.

The quarters consisted of two reinforced concrete bunkers and a brick barracks. One of the bunkers, the smaller of the two, is still intact, the other ruined. There is also the foundation of the large brick-built barracks, which measured 50m × 15m. There are also fragmentary remains of a sewage system and wells. A concrete paved road runs through the grounds. Just behind the complex the railway that used to link the various headquarters still exists and is open seasonally, running between Kętrzyn and Węgorzewo.

It is not known how long Lammers actually spent at 'Wendula' since most of the time he appears to have been at Himmler's *Hochwald*, either in his own train or sharing Himmler's *Heinrich* train.

After the site was abandoned by Lammers in late 1944, it was used during the winter of 1944–45 as a field hospital. Access to the site is free at any time of the year.

The path leading to Lammers' 'Wendula'.

As was the rule with the reinforced bunkers there was at least one other entrance/exit.

The smaller, surviving, bunker at 'Wendula'.

Inside the small bunker.

The large bunker is less accessible than the smaller, intact one.

The larger, ruined, bunker at 'Wendula'.

Inside the large bunker.

Passageway inside the bunker.

The large bunker is well concealed.

Only the foundations and a little of the walls of the barracks are still to be seen at 'Wendula'.

The remains of other brick buildings at 'Wendula'.

Feldquartier, Reichsminister des Auswärtigen, Schloss Steinort

In June 1941, the Lehndorff family castle in Steinort (today the Polish's village of Sztynort) was requisitioned as the field quarters for the Minister of Foreign Affairs (*Reichsminister des Auswärtigen*) of Joachim Ribbentrop. He named his headquarters 'Westphalia' after his train of the same name. The village is picturesquely situated on a promontory near Lake Mauersee, approximately 5½ miles to the south of *Mauerwald*. Ribbentrop's personal guards, some sixty in total, were distributed in underground shelters and around neighbouring localities. It is easily found by following the road southwards from the *Mauerwald* car park for 4.1km to a crossroads, where a left turn leads on to the road that runs past Schloss Steinort another 4.7km to the south-east, at map coordinates 54.131667, 21.684722.

The last hereditary owner of the castle, Heinrich Ahasverus Graf von Lehndorff-Steinort, lived in one wing, while Ribbentrop occupied the other. The greater part of Ribbentrop's several-hundred-strong staff lived at the somewhat distant Sporthotel 'Jägerhöhe' on the Schwenzaitsee.[1] At the time of writing, the castle was undergoing renovation.

Lehndorff-Steinort served during the war as an ordnance officer under General von Bock. He considered the Russian campaign critical, and he was a supporter of Hitler's policies until the death of his brother in July 1941 on the

Joachim von Ribbentrop, seen here stood behind Hitler in the *Wolfsschanze* during an official visit by the Prime Minister of Iraq, Rashid Ali el Gailani, on possibly 15 July 1942.

Schloss Steinort.

An aerial view of the schloss.

Eastern Front and being an eyewitness to the massacre of thousands of Jews at Borisov in Belarus led him to join the resistance movement.

As a first lieutenant in the Reserve Army, Lehndorff-Steinort was assigned to the military district I in Königsberg as a liaison officer for Operation *Valkyrie*. On 19 July 1944 he was notified of the imminent planned assassination attempt.

The following morning, he drove to Königsberg ready to play his part in the coup but when he learned that the attempt had failed, he returned to Steinort, knowing that it would not be long before his involvement would be discovered. On the 21st the Gestapo arrived. He jumped from the first floor into the grounds of the castle but, for the sake of his family, he turned himself in.

He was taken to Gestapo headquarters in Berlin but escaped as he was being taken into the cells on Prinz-Albrecht-Strasse. After four days he reached the area of Neustrelitz in Mecklenburg but was betrayed by a local forester and handed over to the Gestapo. Along with most of the other conspirators, he was executed.

Fremde Heere Ost Hauptquartier, Feste Boyen

The German military intelligence service Foreign Armies East, the *Fremde Heere Ost* (FHO), a department of the OKH, was housed in the nineteenth-century fortress of Boyen. Its purpose was the collection of statistical and technical data on the armies that Germany was at war with or countries that it had planned to invade, deriving most of its information from open sources. It made sense, therefore, for the department to be as close to the enemy as possible. It is situated approximately 34km to the east of the *Wolfsschanze*. In terms of information gathering, the FHO worked alongside, though often in direct competition with, Himmler's SS. One of the FHO's main functions was to provide information each day regarding the locations of all the divisions and army groups of both sides. This information was transferred to a map at *Mauerwald*, which was printed and scrutinised by the OKH and Hitler at the daily situation conferences.

From 1 April 1942, the FHO came under the command of Oberstleutnant Reinhard Gehlen, initially with a staff of thirty-five. Linguists, geographers and anthropologists were subsequently employed to gain a better understanding of the enemy. Gehlen was able to accurately gauge the strength of the Soviet reserve armies, which Hitler repeatedly dismissed as exaggerated only for Gehlen to be proven correct, with disastrous consequences for the German forces.

It was as a result of Hitler's terrible mismanagement of the war that Gehlen was persuaded to join the *Valkyrie* conspiracy. Unlike most of the other conspirators, his involvement was not revealed or suspected, and he survived both the brutal reprisals and the war. As with the other headquarters in East Prussia, Fortress Boyen was abandoned in 1944 as the Red Army approached.

The fortress is still in excellent condition and is open to the public.

Apart from housing the FHO, the fortress was used as a military hospital.

Chapter 7

Führerhauptquartier Werwolf

At 08.15 hours on 16 July 1942, Hitler and his entourage, packed into sixteen aircraft, lifted off from Rastenburg on the long flight south to the Luftwaffe air base at Kalinovka (Kalynivka) in Ukraine to take up residence in what would be the most easterly of the Führer's field headquarters. Work on the site – initially named *Anlage Eichenhain* (Oak Grove), but later renamed *Werwolf*, or *Wehrwolf*, by Hitler – which was situated around 6 miles to the north of Vinnytsia, began in the utmost secrecy in the autumn of 1941, soon after the city had been overrun by German forces, and lasted until June 1942. Polish and Czech workers, as well as local Jews from the nearby village of Stryzhavka, were employed in its construction by Organisation Todt, the hard labour being provided by Soviet prisoners of war. Most of them were killed afterwards to ensure the location of the site remained a secret. They were buried in a mass grave on the opposite side of the Vinnytsia–Zhytomyr road and a monument has since been raised to the estimated 14,000 victims.

According to one report, a rumour had circulated the night before Hitler's arrival that a Russian wearing the uniform of a German major had managed to get into the camp with the aim of killing the Führer. When Hitler leaned of this, he told *Werwolf* Oberstleutnant Thomas, head of the Führer-Begleit-Bataillon and HQ commander, that all the Russians must be shot: 'There is not a moment to lose. They know too much about my HQ.'[1]

Linked to the site, there was a further headquarters for other senior officers to the north of Vinnytsia, at Gulivtsi station. It was named *Steinbruch* (Stone Pit), whilst near Zhytomyr there was Himmler's *Hegewald* (Sanctuary Forest).

When Hitler arrived Thomas was waiting for him. Thomas took Hitler over the terrain around the HQ and showed him the security measures. The area was surrounded by a defensive strip of bunkers linked by an underground tunnel, anti-aircraft guns and tanks, as well as anti-tank ditches and minefields. These positions were manned by a well-armed detachment of Thomas' FBB plus the 4th Heavy Company, 5th Panzer Company, and the eight batteries of Flak Regiment 604.[2] In addition, Rattenhuber, as the man responsible for all Hitler's headquarters, had formed a special group of his RSD whose job was to watch the approaches to the HQ and to keep an eye on the local population.[3]

Construction of one of the three bunkers at *Werwolf* under way in late 1941.

A German staff car pictured by one of the completed bunkers at *Werewolf*.

The *Werwolf* complex was divided into two parts – a central and a general zone, *Sperrkreis* I and II respectively. The central zone was surrounded by a metal fence 2.5m high and surmounted by two rows of razor wire. To provide natural cover and camouflage, some 800 trees and thousands of other shrubs and plants were planted at and around the complex. Approximately 12,000m of ground was laid with grass. Several kilometres of roads and paths were constructed.

Though set in a pine forest measuring approximately 2.5km long and 300m wide, *Werwolf* was nothing remotely like the *Wolfsschanze*, with none of the beauty of the Masuria with its lovely lake and gently rolling hills. Hitler and his staff hated every day of the three months they spent at *Werwolf*. Inside the buildings during the daytime it was hot and stuffy, while at night the log cabins were very cold. The local mosquitoes rivalled those at the *Wolfsschanze* in their numbers and ferocity, but the ones at the *Werwolf* were far more dangerous in that they were the Anopheles strain that carries malaria. Consequently, everyone had to swallow bitter-tasting anti-malaria tablets each evening. But the war against the Soviet Union had reached a critical stage and Hitler wanted to be as close to the fighting as was safely practical.

The surroundings plus the faltering success of the German forces in the East led to frequent arguments between Hitler and his staff, the place being 'plunged in gloom' according to Nicholas von Below: 'Hitler had withdrawn into seclusion. The situation conferences were no longer being held in the Wehrmacht Staff House, but in the large study at Hitler's quarters. When one entered he would not offer his hand but acknowledge the caller's presence by merely extending his arm. He dined alone in his bunker.'[4]

Christa Schroeder accompanied Hitler to the *Werwolf*: 'The living accommodation is similar to the *Wolfsschanze* except we have fortified houses instead of concrete bunkers. They look really attractive but are awfully damp inside ... Daytime temperatures are really high (it is not unusual to have 45–50°C) but at night it is disproportionately cool, and often the weather changes as quick as a flash.'[5]

Hitler's accommodation, his *Führerhaus*, was in *Sperrkreis* I and it consisted of a modest log cabin built around a private courtyard with its own concrete bunker. Being deep in what had recently been enemy territory and potentially at risk from local partisans and fifth-columnists, security was of paramount importance and Rattenhuber had his men search the building's walls for microphones and explosives before Hitler moved in. At the entrance to the site was a sign declaring that the complex was a 'Sanatorium', but such was the presence of so many senior German officials seen in the area – Göring, for instance was chauffeured around in an open-top Mercedes – and with the SS, Gestapo and SD all with a presence in Vinnytsia, this sign would not have fooled anyone for long.

Inhabitants who were permitted to remain in the vicinity of the *Werwolf* were carefully vetted and everyone over the age of 14 was issued with a personal pass that, on pain of death, they had to carry with them at all times.[6]

Felix Hartlaub, a member of the *Wehrmachtführungsstab*, spent time at the *Werwolf*: '*Sperrkreis* I is in the eastern part away from the highway and cordoned off by fencing taller than a man. Across the meadow runs an extensive barbed wire entanglement ... The pines are 20–30 centimetres thick and many have been cut town ... Vegetation from the from the woods is carefully arranged on the roof of the cube-shaped uninhabited [Führer] bunker; on the numerous barracks, camouflage netting is dappled with sea grass. Black ash on the footpaths, fat hydrants, boxes of hose reels on the barrack walls ... At the edge of the wood armoured scout cars keep watch beneath sun-dried camouflage netting.'[7]

The rest of the complex consisted of three small (Class B) bunkers and a total of eighty-one wooden cottages and barracks. Among the buildings was a tea house, a barber's shop, a sauna, a cinema, a bathhouse and three air-raid shelters. There was also, of course, a dining room, which Speer described unflatteringly as 'rather like a railroad station restaurant in a small town'.[8] In addition, there was a personal swimming pool for Hitler and, though he never used it, others did. Among those that used the pool, which measured 15m × 10m, was Christa Schroeder who found the water 'barbarously' cold.[9]

Adjacent to the *Führerhaus* was a building for the shorthand writers who were needed to copy Hitler's directives. Next, inevitably, was Bormann's building, the Reichsleiter making sure, as always, that he controlled all access to the Führer. He was the only person other than Hitler who had his own personal bunker – even Keitel and Jodl had to share.

A substation provided the site's electricity, with overhead wires to the individual buildings. As an emergency back-up three generators were housed in a specifically constructed building. Two 120m-deep artesian wells provided the *Werwolf*'s water supply.[10] Hydrant water was drawn from the Southern Bug (Pivdennyi Buh) river, which is about a kilometre to the west of the complex, and pumped into a large tank. Sewage from the installation was drained into a special purification plant inside the headquarters, and pipes and drainage channels led across to the Bug.[11] The *Werwolf* also had its own vegetable garden, organised by the German horticultural company Ziedenspiner, to provide Hitler with a secure and safe supply of food. This was under the careful direction of his personal chef, SS-Hauptsturmführer Fater, who had to go out and select the vegetables for Hitler himself.[12] According to the historian Anthony Beevor, all other vegetables destined for Hitler's plate had to be dug up under the eyes of an appointed courier, who then took the items directly to the kitchen. The produce was chemically tested before cooking and, as had become mandatory, the food was sampled by one of the food-tasters before being served to the Führer. Such was the degree of

Most of the buildings in the *Werwolf* were timber structures such as the one shown here. Although Hitler had his own bunker, his accommodation was in a hot and stuffy timber building and he soon developed headaches, which did not help his mood or his relationship with his generals.

Hitler shown here, possibly on 20 August 1942, welcoming Otto Thierack, the Reich Minister of Justice, and Justice Minister Kurt Rothenberger.

security, the water from the Bug was tested daily for contamination, intentional or otherwise, and it is alleged that even the returning laundry was X-rayed for suspicious items.[13]

Alexander Stahlberg described the buildings at the *Werwolf* as 'simple and rustic' but admitted that every comfort was provided for inside. Stahlberg, whom it may be recalled was Field Marshal von Manstein's aide-de-camp, also had the opportunity to see Hitler's accommodation. After the Führer had returned to the *Wolfsschanze*, Manstein moved into Hitler's former residence: 'The architect who built this house had designed it with great skill. From the pathway leading to the house it appeared modest, with only two groups of windows on either side of the front door. The two left-hand ones belonging to the Adjutant's room, which I now took over, and the right-hand ones to a living and briefing room which in fact extended backwards like an unfolded towel.'

Hitler's suite, at the back of the building, contained a 'beautiful' living room and study, bedroom and bathrooms. The walls of the suite were covered in pine panelling and decorated with a great many pictures. The prints in Hitler's study were of 'idyllic' scenes by the German romanticist artist Carl Spitzweg and in Hitler's bedroom was a reproduction of a drawing in red chalk showing a young, allegedly Pomeranian, woman, which was hung in such a way that the eyes of the person in bed were inevitably drawn to the portrait. Stahlberg found the woman neither beautiful nor interesting. The fireplace in the living room had a sheet of cast-iron embossed with a representation of the devil dancing in the fires of Hell. Stahlberg described the ground plan of the building's inner courtyard as having been borrowed 'from the classical atriums of the ruined city of Pompeii'.[14]

There was direct telephone link with Berlin, Vinnytsia, the other headquarters, and the Luftwaffe base at Kalinovka, some 20km to the north of *Werwolf*. There was also a daily three-hour flight from Berlin Tempelhof to Kalinovka, and a train service from Berlin-Charlottenburg to the *Werwolf*'s 'Eichenbein' station. This train left Berlin at 19.51 hours each evening, the journey, via Warsaw, Brest-Litovsk, Kovel, Povno and Berditshev taking thirty-four hours, arriving at the *Werwolf* at 06.45 hours on the second morning.[15]

Hitler left the *Werwolf* on 30 October to return to the *Wolfsschanze*. He returned again the following year, between 19 February and 13 March 1943, with his third and final visit taking place on 27 August 1943. He returned to the *Wolfsschanze* on 15 September 1943, and the site was demolished by the retreating German forces in March 1944 under Hitler's express instructions.

The *Werwolf* site has become a visitor attraction, with a visitor centre and museum, and marked pathways through the narrow forest that still surrounds it. There are collections of weapons and military vehicles, including an impressive German Tiger tank, but of the buildings themselves, little is to

The Bulgarian ambassador, Parwan Draganow (second from the left in the foreground), in an audience with Hitler at the *Werwolf* on 14 August 1942. Also present are Otto Meissner, Julius Schaub, Walther Hewel and Paul Schmidt.

Hitler received the Turkish Ambassador to Berlin at the *Werwolf* in August 1942. Present are Joachim von Ribbentrop (first from the right) and Paul Schmidt (first from the left).

Inside the communications centre.

The remains of one of the three bunkers.

The *Werwolf* was very effectively destroyed by German engineers in 1944.

be seen above ground. When Hitler left the *Werwolf* for the last time in August 1943, he ordered the site to be destroyed, insisting that nothing should be left, not even a single piece of furniture, claiming, according to General Warlimont, that any objects the Soviets found would be put on display in Moscow.[16] There is, though, one structure that remains almost as it was more than seventy-five years ago – Hitler's swimming pool. There are marked routes through the site, with some of the buildings being identified.

An view of *Sperrkreis* I of the *Werwolf* showing Hitler's swimming pool.

Chapter 8

Valkyrie – The 20 July 1944 Assassination Attempt on Hitler at the *Wolfsschanze*

To understand the events of 20 July 1944, it is necessary to go back in time to 1938. After taking up the position of Chancellor in 1933, Hitler had set about eliminating any real or perceived opponents. He quickly established control over most public and civilian bodies apart from the Army. The latter's perceived role was that of independent guardian of the state, its political neutrality being enshrined in the oath that every German soldier had to take: 'I swear by God this holy oath that I will at all times, truly and sincerely, serve my people and Fatherland and that oath, as a brave soldier, I will be ready at all times to give my life for this oath.'

Just hours after the death of President Hindenburg on 2 August 1934, and following the removal or resignation of many senior officers, Hitler imposed a new oath, the Law of the Oath of the Wehrmacht, to which again all soldiers had to commit: 'I swear by God this holy oath, that I will give unconditional obedience to the Führer of the German Reich and people, Adolf Hitler, the Supreme Commander of the Wehrmacht and that, as a brave soldier, I will be ready at all times to give my life for this oath.'

Symbolically and literally, Hitler became one with the military. His decisions carried the power of orders. There was no other competing authority to which the military owed allegiance. It was hard for a good, God-fearing German to break such an oath.

Nevertheless, until early 1938, the German Army had largely managed to retain its independence from government. It remained the one major cohesive body that Hitler had limited influence over. That all changed in February 1938. The Commander-in-Chief of the Armed Forces and Minister of War, Generalfeldmarschall Werner von Blomberg, was compelled to resign his post following revelations concerning his recently married wife's long criminal record for prostitution. The man who replaced him, Generaloberst Werner von Fritsch, was also forced to resign due to concocted accusations of homosexuality. Both these generals had voiced their concerns over Hitler's expansionist ambitions and had paid the price.

These 'scandals' enabled Hitler to reorganise the command structure of the German armed forces, placing the Army, Navy and Air Force under a new body, the *Oberkommando der Wehrmacht* (OKW) or Supreme Command of the Armed Forces under Generalfeldmarschall Wilhelm Keitel, while command of the Army was put in the hands of a man that Hitler knew would do his bidding, whether he liked it or not, Generalfeldmarschall Walther von Brauchitsch. At the same time, Hitler ordered the summary retirement of fourteen senior generals. He then replaced Konstantin von Neurath, the Minister of Foreign Affairs, who had also expressed his disapproval of Hitler's policies, with the 'dull but obedient' Joachim von Ribbentrop. The consequence of all these machinations was that if Hitler decided to follow his dream of dominating Central and Eastern Europe, even if that meant inviting war, there was now no one in Germany who could stop him.

With all the power he needed in his own hands, Hitler was ready to take the first step in his plans to create a Greater Germany encompassing all the German-speaking peoples of Central Europe. His first target was Austria. Towards the end of 1918 and into 1919 negotiations had taken place to try and unite Germany and Austria, but this had been blocked by the Allies and, under the terms of the Treaty of Versailles, had been expressly forbidden. As he had already broken the terms of the Treaty in March 1936 by remilitarising the Ruhr, creating an air force and expanding the army, with little opposition from Britain and France, Hitler was confident he could absorb Austria into the Third Reich without fear of repercussion.

Consequently, on 12 March 1938, German troops crossed the border, being greeted by cheering crowds and Nazi salutes. The Anschluss (joining) was legitimised by the Austrian Government and confirmed in a plebiscite four weeks later, in which 99.7 per cent of voters agreed to the union with Germany.

The world held its collective breath to see what the response of Britain and France would be to the Anschluss. The answer was soon forthcoming, with British Prime Minister Neville Chamberlain conceding that 'nothing could have arrested what has actually happened [in Austria] unless this country and other countries had been prepared to use force', and no one was prepared to use force. Hitler had gambled on Allied acquiescence and had won.

His next move was to dismantle Czechoslovakia, the artificially constructed state to the east of Germany that had been carved from the former Austro-Hungarian Empire. Within its borders were two important features. One was the Sudetenland, where more than 3 million ethnic Germans lived, the other was the Skoda Works, which had previously been the principal arms manufacturer for the Austro-Hungarian armed forces and one of the finest in Europe. Hitler intended to seize both.

Many senior figures in Germany were extremely worried by Hitler's policies. A number of high-ranking civilian individuals actually approached both London and Paris repeatedly in a bid to enlist support for their opposition to Hitler. Though these envoys were received by ministry officials in both countries, it was with much distrust. If they were not secretly working with Hitler in some fashion, then their suggestions that Britain and France should support the overthrow of the legitimate German government was politically beyond the pale. All such approaches were rejected.[1]

Nevertheless, opposition among officers in the German Army was growing. Added to what they perceived as the disgraceful treatment of Blomberg and Fritsch was the fear that Hitler was leading the county to disaster. Though relieved that Britain and France had accepted the Anschluss with little fuss, they could not believe that these two nations would sit on their hands if Hitler invaded an independent sovereign country. Hitler would have to be removed from office – by whatever means – before he could move against Czechoslovakia.

It was the day after Fritsch had been forced to resign, when Generaloberst Ludwig Beck, Chief of the General Staff, met with Admiral Wilhelm Canaris, head of the Abwehr (the German military intelligence service) and his deputy, Oberstleutnant Hans Oster. They agreed that Hitler had to be stopped and began to plot the Führer's downfall. But three men alone could not topple the Nazi Party, so Oster sent 'missionaries' to the headquarters of the twelve military districts into which Germany was divided to garner support. No coup could succeed in toppling the Government if it was opposed by the commanders of the military districts. Equally important was that another civil administration was ready to step into the vacuum created by the removal of the Nazi leadership. So, drawn into what would become known as the 'Oster Conspiracy', were a number of important individuals, including Han-Bernd Gisevius, former member of the Gestapo and employee of the Ministry of the Interior; Carl Goerdeler, former mayor of Leipzig; and Hjalmar Schacht, a former minister of economics and the then current president of the Reichsbank.

These men still hoped that such extreme action would not be necessary and that if the politicians in France and Great Britain stood firm and frustrated Hitler's territorial aims there was a chance that opposition groups in Germany could oust the Führer peacefully. Everything depended on how the Allied leaders would act over the course of the next few months, as Hitler increased his rhetoric over the alleged 'plight' of the Sudeten Germans, who were under-represented in the Czech parliament and suffered considerably higher levels of unemployment than their Czech counterparts.

Since the Anschluss, the Sudeten Germans, claiming to be a persecuted minority, had been agitating noisily for their own union with the Third Reich. The leader of the Sudeten German Party, the Sudentendeutsche Partei, Konrad Henlein, demanded autonomy for the region, which the Czech Government could not accept.

As the manufactured crisis escalated, Hitler told his generals to prepare to attack Czechoslovakia no later than 2 October. This prompted Generaloberst

Beck to submit a memorandum to von Brauchitsch predicting a move against Czechoslovakia would lead to a protracted and costly war, warning that 'Germany is not fit for a long war.' Brauchitsch dare not be seen by Hitler as condoning Beck's negative views and the memo was not passed on to the German leader.

On 19 May 1938, German forces were observed massing on the Czech border. Two days later the Czechs mobilised. Britain and France issued stern communiques, threatening that a move against Czechoslovakia might result in a 'European conflagration'. Much to the surprise of the Western leaders, Hitler did not call their bluff, and von Ribbentrop was able, for once, to tell the truth (but not the whole truth) when he assured them that Germany was not on the verge of invading Czechoslovakia. He did not say what might happen in the future.

But the threats that had emanated from Paris and London further reinforced the conviction of the Oster group that when, for it was no longer if, Hitler invaded Czechoslovakia, Britain, France and probably the Soviet Union, would declare war on Germany.

Beck tried again to point out the risks he believed that Hitler was running in planning to occupy Czechoslovakia, but his advice was dismissed out of hand by the Führer, who was becoming increasingly annoyed with the Chief of Staff's pessimism. For his part, Beck saw that his efforts to deter Hitler with reasoned analysis had failed and he became more convinced than ever that the only way of preventing another European war was by removing Hitler.

Throughout June and July, diplomatic efforts by British Foreign Secretary Lord Halifax and Prime Minister Neville Chamberlain appeared to be bearing fruit as tensions eased after the May crisis. Indeed, towards the end of July Chamberlain had managed to persuade the Czech Government and the Sudetens to agree to a British mediator, a shipping magnate called Lord Runciman. The situation, Chamberlain now believed, was under control. Germany, meanwhile, prepared for war.

Aware that the date of Hitler's proposed invasion was drawing closer, Beck took steps that could, quite reasonably, be considered treasonable. On 4 August, for the first and only time in the history of the Third Reich, the Army's senior generals met without having been summoned by the Führer. The Chief of Staff had called them together to present them with his apocalyptic view of what would happen if Germany invaded Czechoslovakia. He hoped that he could convince them to refuse to carry out Hitler's instructions. There was a degree of unanimity among the generals, with much consideration given to them resigning en masse. Mutiny was in the air. Only two generals rebuked the others for their treacherous words, and one of them, General Walther von Reichenau, went off to tell Hitler all that had transpired.

The Führer responded by convening his own meeting with the military hierarchy on 15 August. Hitler was nothing if he was not persuasive, and he convinced many of the generals that neither Britain nor France would lift a finger to help the Czechs. Beck was unmoved by Hitler's words, but he now saw that nothing he could say would stop the invasion. If words were not enough, then possibly deeds might. So the Chief of Staff of the Army resigned.

Beck hoped that others would follow but the naturally conservative officers baulked at taking such an extreme measure. Even Beck's replacement, Generaloberst Franz Halder, who had previously called Hitler a 'madman' and a 'criminal', now vacillated. The cautious generals decided to wait and see what would happen.

Beck, and the group that had gathered around himself and Oster, now knew that they were on their own. They also knew that without the support of the other generals they could no longer openly conspire against Hitler.

Time was running out for the resisters to draw the men necessary for a successful coup into the conspiracy. One man they were able to recruit, and possibly the most important, was General Erwin von Witzleben, commander of III Military District, within whose jurisdiction was the Berlin Defence District.

Of paramount importance was a defiant stand by the British. If Chamberlain made it abundantly clear that the invasion of Czechoslovakia would result in a declaration of war against Germany, Hitler would have to stand down his army and the myth of the Führer's brilliant political manoeuvring would be dispelled. The task of explaining this to the British Government was handed to the influential monarchist, Ewald von Kleist-Schmenzin: 'Bring me certain proof that England will fight if Czechoslovakia is attacked,' he was told by Oster before he left Berlin, 'and I will make an end of this regime.'

Exactly how Hitler was to be disposed of when the time for action arrived was the subject of much discussion. An outright assassination was repugnant to many of the officers, most preferring to see Hitler arrested and tried for the many crimes his regime had committed against the German people, or even declared insane by a panel of doctors and committed to an asylum.

The plan eventually agreed upon was that von Witzleben would march to the Chancellery with a squad of young officers and Abwehr agents under Major Friedrich Wilhelm Heinz. If Hitler's SS guards attempted to stop Heinz's men from entering the Chancellery, they would be shot. Witzleben would demand Hitler's resignation. If he refused, Hitler would be arrested and taken to a secret location where he would be held until the coup had been completed. What many of the conspirators did not know was that Heinz believed that: 'Hitler alive has more weight than all the troops at our disposal,' and had decided that he would engineer a situation of some kind that would result in a gun battle in which the Führer would be killed.

In preparation for the assault upon the Chancellery, Admiral Canaris took guns and explosives (to blow in the doors of the Chancellery if necessary) from the Abwehr arsenal and secreted them in 'safe houses' around Berlin for Heinz's assault squad.

The conspirators now waited on the response to a final mission to London. Kleist met Lord Lloyd, an outspoken critic of Hitler, and Sir Robert Vansittart, Permanent Under-Secretary at the Foreign Office, advising them that the invasion of Czechoslovakia was a certainty unless Britain took decisive action. 'The mobilisation plans are complete, zero day is fixed, and the Army group commanders have their orders. All will run according to plan at the end of September, and no one can stop it unless Britain speaks an open warning to Herr Hitler.'

Vansittart took this information to Lord Halifax, who in turn passed it on to Chamberlain. None of these politicians saw anything other than Kleist as being the representative of a group that merely sought power in Germany for its own ends. To Chamberlain they were merely a 'gang of traitors'.

Hans Oster, meanwhile, had been rapidly extending his network, and had his spies in government ministries and the police. Even General Halder, who saw the date of the invasion of Czechoslovakia looming, declared he would back the coup, but only if Hitler issued the order to attack the Czechs. One man who remained outside the conspiracy was Brauchitsch. If the senior Army commander could be persuaded to counter Hitler's orders, there would be no invasion, war would be averted, and the Führer's authority permanently held in check. Though he was told that: 'the destiny of the German army and thus the destiny of the German people' lay in his hands, Brauchitsch remained unmoved.

Also unmoved was the situation between Berlin and Prague. The Sudetens continued to demonstrate for the Sudetenland to be ceded to Germany and towards the end of August Lord Runciman had to confess that he was unable to reconcile the differences between Konrad Henlein and the Czech President, Edvard Beneš. The Germany Army was also conducting manoeuvres close to the border with Czechoslovakia. It seemed the repeated warnings that Hitler was set on seizing the Sudetenland by force were all too true.

Chamberlain called an emergency Cabinet meeting on 30 August. Only one item was on the agenda for that day – should Britain announce that it would go to war to uphold Czechoslovakia's sovereignty? The arguments for and against such a declaration were obvious to all. But no one could predict what would happen if Britain did take such a bold step. Would Hitler back down, or would Europe be flung into a terrible war with Germany? Like Hitler's generals, Chamberlain's ministers decided to wait and see.

Oddly, this was exactly what Chamberlain wanted, for he had a scheme to write his name in the history books as the man who brought peace to the troubled Continent. It was termed 'Plan Z'. Chamberlain suspected that if Britain did not threaten to go to war with Germany, Hitler would continue his preparations against the Czechs. So, just as the Germans were on the verge of launching their attack, Chamberlain would fly, unannounced, to meet the Führer and save the day with a typically British compromise.

Oster, meanwhile, continued with his own plans, which included an approach to Count Helldorf, the President of the Berlin Police. Such a move had to be taken with extreme care, for his loyalties remained untested. It was Han Bernd Gisevius who made the approach and to his immense relief, Helldorf was willing to act with the conspirators. Oster could now be certain of securing Berlin, with the Army and now the police under his orders, and detailed plans for the coup were drawn up during the second week of September. Certain key buildings would have to be seized on the day of the coup, but it was thought most government departments would accept the change of regime with little fuss, and that after a brief period of military rule to ensure the leading Nazis were rounded up, the country could be handed back to the civilians. The SS would resist, of course, but there was just one SS division in existence at that time, and this alone could not stop the coup.

Everyone now waited for the signal that would see Major Heinz's assault squad storm the Reich Chancellery. That signal was the implementation of Hitler's 'Plan Green', the invasion of Czechoslovakia. Halder would be given at least twenty-four hours' notice to enable him to issue his instructions to his corps commanders – twenty-four hours to topple Hitler and his hated regime before Europe was plunged into war.

But then it happened. On 14 September, the British Prime Minister sent a message to Hitler telling the Führer that he was flying to Germany the next day to offer a solution, once and for all, to the Czech problem.

Hitler decided to meet Chamberlain at the Berghof, his lovely Alpine retreat above the Bavarian market town of Berchtesgaden, and arrangements were rapidly made to receive the British Prime Minister, who was taking his first ever flight in an aeroplane. The two leaders met face to face in a small study in the Berghof with Hitler's interpreter the only other person present. At a recent Nuremberg rally, Hitler had called for a plebiscite in the Sudetenland to determine if its people wanted to remain part of Czechoslovakia or join the Third Reich. Hitler asked Chamberlain if he supported the principle of self-determination. In response, Chamberlain said that, 'It was immaterial ... whether the Sudeten Germans stayed in Czechoslovakia.' Hitler was going to be given what he wanted.

Chamberlain returned to advise his Cabinet of the meeting with the German Chancellor, following which Lord Halifax discussed the Prime Minister's proposal with the French and the Czechs. The French had agreed that if the majority of the Sudetens wanted to join Germany then they should be allowed to. President Beneš was given no choice.

It seemed to the conspirators that Hitler was going to have his way and that war would be avoided. But then Hitler made further demands, that the Polish and Hungarian minorities in Czechoslovakia should also be granted the right of self-determination and that any plebiscites would only take place after the German Army had marched into Czechoslovakia. This amounted to the forced dismemberment of the country – this, surely, could never be agreed to by Britain and France? Hitler was clearly bent on war.

This drove even more senior figures into the Oster conspiracy. Heinz and his men were poised for action. Chamberlain was not.

With Hitler declaring that the German Army would march into Czechoslovakia on 1 October unless his demands were met, Chamberlain held a third meeting with the Führer on 29 September initiated by the Italian dictator Benito Mussolini. In the early hours of the following day, Chamberlain and Hitler, plus Mussolini and the French Prime Minister, Édouard Daladier, signed the Munich Agreement that gave the Sudetenland to Germany and, effectively, gave Hitler control over the fate of the rest of Czechoslovakia. In return for Chamberlain's compliance over Czechoslovakia, Hitler agreed to sign a peace treaty with Britain. Both men believed they had achieved everything they had set out to accomplish.

Chamberlain returned to London, driving through crowds that cheered and waved as he drove to Buckingham Palace to brief the King. He then returned to 10 Downing Street, where he famously declared to the exultant throng he had achieved 'peace with honour ... peace for our time'.

The rejoicing of the people in Britain was more than matched by that of the German *volk*. Hitler would never be more popular than at this moment. As the German tanks rolled across the Czech border into Sudetenland unopposed on 1 October, the conspirators knew that there was no longer any hope of mounting a coup against the Führer. Oster, Gisevius, and Schacht met at Witzleben's house, where they tossed 'their lovely plans and projects into the fire'.

Chamberlain believed he had saved Europe. In reality, it was Hitler he had saved.

The apparent moral capitulation by France and Great Britain over Czechoslovakia led to, rather than deterred, a European war. Hitler doubted that the Western Powers would throw themselves into an armed conflict with Germany; the horrors of the Great War were still too vividly remembered. He felt confident that he could take Poland just as he had Czechoslovakia and Britain and France would again accept a fait accompli.

His judgement, though, was flawed, and two days after German forces had invaded Poland on 1 September 1939, France and Great Britain declared war on Germany – just as the opposition figures had feared. What they had not anticipated, however, was the staggering success of the German forces that rolled across Poland and then overran Denmark and Norway in April 1940, followed by the invasion of France and the Low Countries in May. Even the most sceptical military men had to concede that Hitler's seemingly reckless rush into war had achieved results far beyond anything the more conservative generals had imagined possible.

Though the group opposed to Hitler still wished to see him removed from power, such was the Führer's popularity and that of the Nazi regime, there was every likelihood that the German people would not support a coup. Hans Oster and others had no choice but to adopt a 'wait-and-see' approach, and while they waited German forces invaded the Soviet Union in June 1941.

At that time, the atmosphere at the headquarters of the OKW was one of great optimism, but that soon evaporated in the vast, unconquerable, Russian steppes. As the war against the Soviet Union entered its second year, the mood among Army officers began to change. Defeat was in the air and many were exasperated with Hitler's handling of the war. Increasing numbers of officers saw that the only chance of avoiding a complete catastrophe was by removing Hitler.

There was also another element that drove more men into the conspiracy – that of the barbarity with which the campaign in the East was being conducted, particularly against civilians who were victims of arbitrary deportation and summary execution on a vast scale. Orders were issued to German commanders that 'partisans are to be ruthlessly eliminated in battle or during attempts to escape', and all attacks by the civilian population against Wehrmacht soldiers were to be 'suppressed by the army on the spot by using extreme measures, till [the] annihilation of the attackers'. The instructions issued by the *Oberkommando der Wehrmacht* included the statement that: 'Every officer in the German occupation in the East of the future will be entitled to perform execution(s) without trial, without any formalities, on any person suspected of having a hostile attitude towards the Germans.'

These measures and the treatment of innocent, unarmed civilians and of helpless prisoners of war appalled many German officers. Some, who had reluctantly tolerated the extremes of the Nazi Party now found themselves being repelled with what they witnessed. Ordinary decent men also saw themselves being implicated in these excesses by association.

It was the officers of the Army who saw that it was up to them to put a stop to these horrors and the only way this could be achieved was by assassinating Hitler. It was at this point in the story that one promising young officer comes to the fore – Oberstleutnant Hermann Henning Karl Robert von Tresckow.

Born in Magdeburg, von Tresckow was the son of cavalry general and was steeped in the Prussian military tradition. Initially impressed with Hitler's militarism, by 1938 Tresckow was another of those who saw the Nazi leader was going to drag his country into a calamitous war. There was, of course, no means by which he could influence events and once the fighting began in 1939, as a patriotic German, he put all his endeavours into securing a German victory.

As first a General Staff officer (Ia) of Army Group Centre, Tresckow was well aware of the crimes that were being perpetrated against the Poles and the Russians. Serving at Headquarters also meant that he had contact with the senior officers of the Army Group and was able to quietly learn which of them were as shocked as he was at what was happening.

He also sent one of his adjutants, Leutnant Fabian von Schlabrendorff, to Berlin to see if Ludwig Beck, or anyone else of such standing, was still willing to act against Hitler. Schlabrendorff did indeed find that the group around Oster and Canaris continued to seek a means by which Hitler could be deposed. He later discovered that General der Infanterie Friedrich Olbricht, Chief of the General Army Office in the OKH, also wished to see Hitler, whose strategic decisions were proving increasingly disastrous, removed from power. Knowing that there were such powerful figures willing to support him, Tresckow felt confident that he could make a move against Hitler that just might precipitate the collapse of the entire the rotten Nazi regime.

Tresckow could not take such action unless his commanding officer was in league with the conspirators. Generalfeldmarschall von Bock, though, was not prepared to be drawn into such an act, especially as Hitler remained immensely popular across Germany.

A reversal of German fortunes on the battlefield, as many had believed was inevitable, gave Tresckow his opportunity. During the winter of 1941–42, the Soviets mounted a counter-offensive that saw the German army suffer its first defeats of the war. Buoyed by expectations of continued success, the sudden setback in the East came as a severe blow to the people of the Reich. This had two beneficial effects for the conspirators. The first was that Hitler's popularity waned for the first time in many years and the second was that Bock was replaced by Generalfeldmarschall Günther von Kluge, who had been against Hitler's occupation of the Sudetenland in 1938 and had argued against the attack upon France and the Low Countries in 1940. Though Kluge was unwilling to plot against Hitler in the midst of a titanic struggle against the Soviets, Tresckow knew that he was free to plan the demise of Hitler without fear of being denounced.

In the summer of 1943, Hitler launched Operation *Zitadelle* against the Soviets. It proved to be a disaster, with more than 200,000 men being killed, wounded or taken prisoner. In addition, the Germans lost around 1,400 tanks and artillery pieces, while some 800 aircraft were destroyed or severely damaged. Any lingering belief in Germany emerging from the war victorious died along with its young men on the bloody fields of Kursk, 280 miles to the south-west of Moscow. Winter brought with it a Soviet counter-offensive that saw the German forces being pushed back for 500 miles.

Far to the south, British and US forces had invaded Italy, and Hitler's once favourite ally, Mussolini, had been overthrown. German troops had been sent into Italy to halt the Western Allies, and, with the very real prospect of an imminent invasion of northern Europe, Hitler was faced with fighting a war not on two, but three, fronts. The conspirators knew that Hitler had to be removed, and quickly, before Germany was destroyed.

It was one thing wishing to see the end of Hitler and his dysfunctional regime, but how to accomplish such an objective was something altogether different. As it happened, there was already a mechanism in place for a temporary seizure of all key government agencies. This was Operation *Valkyrie*, which was a plan designed to react to an emergency in the form of internal revolt by the many thousands of foreign workers in Germany or an attempt to take over the government. On the issuing of the *Valkyrie* order to the Reserve Army, which was based in the Berlin area, the troops would immediately occupy and protect all government buildings and communications installations. It also established emergency military control over civilian authorities.

The conspirators therefore aimed to assassinate Hitler and then use the Reserve Army through the *Valkyrie* order to take control of Berlin. Once the Reserve Army had taken control, a proclamation would be issued announcing the death of Hitler and of the formation of a new provisional government. There was likely to be resistance from the SS, the Gestapo and senior Nazi Party officials, but it was expected that the swift seizure of power by the Army would neutralise their efforts. The new government would quickly contact the Allied governments in a bid to end the war and save Germany from destruction.

The one great obstacle to this plan was that, as Commander-in-Chief, only Hitler, or if he was in some way incapacitated, the man at the head of the Reserve Army, Generaloberst Friedrich Fromm, could issue the *Valkyrie* order. Somehow, the conspirators needed to find both someone in Berlin who could activate these schemes under the guise of the official *Valkyrie* arrangements and a person to assassinate the Führer. This they found in one person – the now famous, or infamous, Oberst Claus von Stauffenberg.

Stauffenberg, the son of a count, fought loyally for his country and its fascist regime throughout the early part of the war, being severely wounded serving in North Africa, losing his left eye, his right hand, and two fingers on his left hand. It was only around the turn of the year 1941–42 that he first began to express negative views about the leadership of his country. This was when he was talking to his cousin, Hans Christoph Stauffenberg, who had cautiously reached out to him on behalf of the opposition. Hans reported that: 'I have spoken to Claus. He says that we have to win the war first.'

This was supported by General der Panzertruppe. Hermann Balck, who had frequent personal and official contact with Stauffenberg: 'As long as I was a member of the High Command of the Army, Stauffenberg was to my knowledge no opponent of the system. He strove, like the rest of us, to bring matters to a good end.'

Stauffenberg slowly came to be opposed to Hitler and the way in which the war was being fought, feelings which began on 20 January 1942. It was on that day that Stauffenberg noted in his diary that the organisational department of the general staff announced a shortage of 93,000 men for the Eastern

Front army. As some 800,000 reinforcements had been sent to Russia, this meant that Germany had lost almost 900,000 men since the invasion of the Soviet Union on 22 June 1941. If that trend was to continue the German army would be wiped out. Stauffenberg was also aware that there were only around 200 serviceable tanks on the Eastern Front.

As the war progressed, Stauffenberg, as a staff officer and privy to the hard facts, came to the conclusion – the very obvious conclusion – that unless the conduct of the war was taken out of Hitler's hands, Germany was doomed to catastrophic defeat. By August of 1942, Stauffenberg spoke openly for the first time of making peace while Germany was still in a strong bargaining position.

There was, therefore, no time to lose. The sooner the assassination attempt could be made, the greater the impact, and there was still hope that the death of Hitler would enable the new administration to renounce the policies of the Nazi Party to the world as an aberration and beg the Allies to save Germany – a new democratic and peace-loving Germany that had finally thrown off the shackles of a detested dictator. This could not happen if the leading Nazis stepped into Hitler's shoes. There had to be a complete overthrow of the existing regime. The only chance, the only possible chance, of avoiding a complete calamity was to depose Hitler and all his senior henchmen without delay.

The first scheme to assassinate Hitler devised by Tresckow and Stauffenberg was to plant explosives disguised as two bottles of Cointreau in Hitler's plane as it flew back to Rastenburg after a visit to Army Group Centre Headquarters at Smolensk, on 13 March 1943. The bomb was carried on to the aircraft unwittingly by one of Hitler's entourage and placed in the hold. In Berlin, Goerdeler, General Beck and others who were to form the new provisional government following Hitler's demise, waited expectantly for the news of the plane crash. But Hitler's Condor arrived safely at Rastenburg, the bomb having failed to detonate.

The failed bomb attempt in no way diminished von Tresckow's and Stauffenberg's resolve. Just eight days later, on 21 March, another opportunity presented itself and Tresckow did not hesitate. Hitler was scheduled to view an exhibition of captured Soviet equipment and weapons at the Armoury in Berlin, and Army Group Centre was asked to send a representative who could answer any questions the Führer might have. This was an unexpected chance to get close to Hitler and another member of the conspiracy, Rudolf Christoph von Gersdorff, an Army Group Centre liaison officer with the Abwehr, volunteered to plant a bomb that would finish off the Führer. However, Gersdorff found that the Armoury was too heavily guarded to allow him the opportunity to conceal the bomb. He decided that the only way he could accomplish his mission was to blow himself up as he stood next to the Führer.

On the day in question, as Hitler approached the exhibition, Gersdorff set the fuse, placed the bomb in his uniform pocket and waited his opportunity to end Hitler's reign of terror. But instead of lingering to inspect the weapons, Hitler walked briskly through the exhibition room and outside into the street. Seeing his chance gone, but with the acid of the fuse still burning in his pocket, Gersdorff had to dash into a toilet to disarm the bomb with just moments to spare.

The next scheme devised by the conspirators was in November 1943, and it was Axel von Bussche who had been drawn into the conspiracy after witnessing the shocking massacre of some 12,000 Jews at Dubno in the Ukraine, who volunteered to undertake a mission that could not fail to kill the Führer – a suicide mission.

The German troops had suffered terribly from the weather during the first two winters of the war in the Soviet Union, having been ill-equipped for the harsh conditions. In particular, they lacked suitable clothing, many having to fight, and freeze, in their summer uniforms. The design of new winter uniforms for the Heer was therefore of interest to Hitler and he was to be given a personal viewing of the clothing at the *Wolfsschanze* – and the man who would model the uniform for Hitler was Major Bussche. It was understood that both Himmler and Göring would also attend the viewing, allowing for the possibility of eliminating the top three Nazis with a single blow.

Axel Bussche was regarded as exemplifying the true 'Nordic' racial type so beloved by Hitler and the Nazis. He was over 2m tall, blond and blue-eyed, and had served with distinction on the Eastern Front, being awarded a cluster of medals including the Iron Cross First Class – the perfect model for the new uniform.

Stauffenberg arranged for Bussche to join him at *Mauerwald*, where he handed Bussche a British bomb known as a Clam, containing approximately 200g of TNT in a plastic body with a No. 27 detonator. The advantage the Clam offered was that its fuse was silent compared with the hissing noise made by the German counterpart. Its main disadvantage was that it was activated by acid from a vial that took ten minutes to eat through the fuse before it detonated the explosive. Such a time lapse was considered too great a risk. Hitler changed his plans so frequently and unpredictably that he might well have left the room long before the bomb detonated. What was needed was a device that detonated almost instantaneously. This was found in the form of the fuse of a German hand grenade that exploded in 4.5 seconds after activation. In those few seconds, Bussche believed he could muffle the unavoidable sound of the hissing by coughing or clearing his throat.

Having decided on the detonator, explosives had to be obtained. A staff officer could not simply ask for a quantity of explosives without questions being asked. So, through a somewhat convoluted process, another conspirator, Major Gerhard Knaak, managed to procure a 1kg charge. He handed this to fellow plotter Leutnant Albrecht von Hagen, who passed it onto Leutnant Helmut von Gottberg of Infantry Regiment No. 9. Gottberg took the explosive and a hand grenade casing to Bussche, who was in Potsdam. Bussche, with the help of Gottberg, then constructed a suitable fuse mechanism, as described by Peter Hoffman: 'He sawed the haft of the grenade in two, leaving the part containing the fuse, and he unscrewed the primer. He shortened the draw thread which ran down inside the haft, leaving the pull-button so that there was very little play between the button and the haft. In this way only a very small pulling motion would be required instead of the more extensive movement normally necessary. The hand grenade fuse fitted well into the pioneer charge. The whole thing could well be concealed in one of the deep pockets of the wide trousers then normally worn.'[2] Bussche planned to pull on the button, count a few seconds and then leap forward and grab Hitler as the bomb exploded.

Everything was then set for the modelling of the new uniform for 16 November but, once again, circumstances saved Hitler. The night before the demonstration the railway truck carrying the new uniforms to the front was destroyed in an RAF bombing raid on Berlin. For the next two days Bussche remained nervously at the *Wolfsschanze*, fearing that his bomb would be detected, before, on the 18th, he was allowed to return to his unit.[3]

As the plot had not been uncovered, when the viewing of the uniforms was scheduled for 11 February 1944, Bussche again volunteered to carry out the bombing. But in January he was seriously wounded, losing one of his legs. Undeterred by this setback, another officer stepped forward. Lieutenant Ewald-Heinrich von Kleist-Schmenzin, son of Generalfeldmarschall Ewald von Kleist, volunteered to take Bussche's place. However, the situation on the Eastern Front became increasingly critical for the Germans and, with more pressing matters to deal with than uniforms, the demonstration was repeatedly postponed and finally cancelled.

Though the suicide attempts had not proved possible, the conspirators still sought to assassinate Hitler, and they still had the explosive in their possession. This 1kg of British Haxonite was hidden at *Mauerwald* along with the plans for the overthrow of the Reich following Hitler's death. Obviously, it was dangerous to be found in possession of such material and the risk of discovery was high given the high level of security that was maintained at the OKH headquarters. Rather than leave such incriminating material in one of the buildings, therefore, Kuhn and Hagen decided to bury the explosive and detonators in the woods under one of the wooden watchtowers (where their location could be easily remembered) and the documents in a separate spot, all within the perimeter boundary of the *Wolfsschanze*. Burying it in the grounds of the *Wolfsschanze* meant that the explosive was near at hand – and its ownership anonymous.

As it transpired, on the night they tried to bury the explosive and the documents, the two men were spotted digging in the dark by a guard patrol of the Geheime Feldpolizei. A tracker dog was let off its leash and the explosive was discovered. Fortunately, Kuhn and Hagen escaped unrecognised and the incriminating documents were not uncovered. The Geheime Feldpolizei turned the explosive over to the Army to complete the investigation. Fortunately, Oberstleutnant Werner Schrader was put in charge of the investigation by Oberst Radke. Schrader was a close friend of Hans Oster – and thus a conspirator was put in charge of investigating the conspiracy![4] Schrader succeeded in delaying and hampering the investigation, and he ensured that the perpetrators were never identified. In fact, he even managed to split the explosive into two, with one half being returned to Major Kuhn and the conspirators.

Following these setbacks, Stauffenberg decided that he would have to take matters into his one, disfigured, hand.

Stauffenberg had proven to be a very capable organiser with the General Army Office in Berlin's Bendlerblock and, on 1 July 1944, he was promoted and transferred to the Reserve Army as its Chief of Staff, making him General Fromm's deputy. Fromm was frequently summoned to briefings with Hitler to which Stauffenberg would be expected to attend. Everything had seemingly fallen into place. Stauffenberg would have unfettered access to the Führer, and he would be the one who would kill the German leader.

When he was informed that Hitler wanted to see him at the Berghof to discuss the movement of fifteen newly formed grenadier divisions to the Eastern Front to try and hold back the Russian advance, he knew that his chance had come. On 11 July 1944, Stauffenberg flew down to Berchtesgaden with explosives in his briefcase, notifying his co-conspirators that he was about to act. Consequently, the key conspirators once again stood ready in Berlin to undertake their roles in the coup.

Everything was set, all were prepared. Stauffenberg had taken explosives with him to the Berghof five days earlier, on 6 July, possibly to see how practical an assassination attempt might be. This time he fully intended to carry out the task he had been destined to perform. Nothing happened.

Stauffenberg, after discussions with some of the other conspirators, decided that Himmler and Göring must also be eliminated at the same time as Hitler so that there was no possibility of either of these characters being able to mount a successful claim to the leadership of the country. Neither were present and Stauffenberg, and his explosives, returned to Berlin.

Stauffenberg knew that he had become a trusted individual and that he could carry explosives in his briefcase without being searched. He also knew that another opportunity would present itself in time – and that time came just four days later.

On 15 July, Stauffenberg flew to another meeting with Hitler, but this time at the *Wolfsschanze*. Once again he carried his briefcase in which were two 1kg slabs of plastic explosives hidden under a spare shirt.

Claus von Stauffenberg is seen here standing to the left of General Karl Bodenschatz, who is shaking hands with Hitler on 15 July 1944, when the assassination attempt so nearly took place. The group is standing near the *Lagebaracke*, with the Guest Bunker, Building No. 6, in the background.

After breakfast with Keitel, he attended a succession of short meetings in Hitler's conference room but, as on 11 July, neither Himmler nor Göring were present, so, when he had the chance, Stauffenberg slipped away to call Berlin. He was told to carry out the assassination regardless.

Stauffenberg returned to the conference room determined at last to blow Hitler to Hell only to find his suitcase missing! As he frantically looked round the room, fellow conspirator Generalmajor Helmuth Stieff walked in with the briefcase. There was now no opportunity to set the fuse, and Hitler left the room to live for another few days.

So certain had the conspirators been that this time the assassination would happen, orders for Phase One of *Valkyrie* had already been issued, and troops were on the move to take control of the key installations in Berlin. These orders had to be quickly cancelled before any of Hitler's acolytes learnt of it.

The conspirators knew that they could not risk another such failure. Fortunately, on 19 July, Stauffenberg was ordered to meet Hitler the following day, this time to bring the Führer up to date with the state of preparedness of the fifteen new divisions he had earlier been told to cobble together from the shrinking number of available troops. After the debacle of 15 July, it had been agreed that the assassination would take place whether Himmler or Göring were present or not without further consultation.

Stauffenberg woke early on the morning of 20 July 1944 to prepare for what was to be a day that would live forever in history. Once washed, shaved and dressed, he was met by his driver, Corporal Karl Schweizer, who had delivered not one but two identical bomb-laden briefcases to Stauffenberg the previous afternoon from their place of safe-keeping in the hands of Colonel Fritz von der Lancken. This time there could be no mistake.

Along with Stauffenberg's brother, Berthold, the two men were taken by Schweizer in the staff car to Rangsdorf airport, and were met by Stauffenberg's aide, and fellow conspirator Werner von Haeften and his brother, Bernt. They boarded the courier plane of another of the conspirators, the Quartermaster General of the Army (Kurierflugzeug des Generalquartiermeisters des Heeres) Eduard Wagner. Also taking the flight to the *Wolfsschanze* were Generalmajor Hellmuth Stieff and his aide, Major Roll, who were on their way to *Mauerwald*. The aircraft took off just after 07.00 hours.[5]

The Heinkel He 111 landed at Rastenburg shortly after 10.00 hours, and the party on board were taken by staff car to the *Wolfsschanze*. Stauffenberg then had breakfast with the adjutant of the camp commandant, Captain Leonhard von Möllendorff, in *Casino* 2 of *Sperrkreis* I.

At 11.00 hours Stauffenberg attended his first meeting of the day, which was with the Chief of the Organisations Section of the OKW General der Infanterie Walther Buhle, and others, before briefing Keitel on the state of the fifteen new divisions in the OKW bunker in *Sperrkreis* I.

Kurt Salterberg claims to have been on duty that morning at the entrance of the Führer Restricted Zone. He remembered that Stauffenberg and a number of other officers arrived at his post along with Keitel who, 'showed me his valid permanent ID from about three meters away, after which the entire group could enter the inner restricted area'. Salterberg's post was just 20–30m away from the conference barracks.

Stauffenberg carried the papers he needed for his meeting with Keitel in his pocket. Due to his junior rank, Haeften was not permitted into the meeting and had to wait in an adjoining room or, as some accounts state, in the corridor outside. Seemingly, Staff Sergeant Werner Vogel, Keitel's aide, noticed the nervous-looking Haeften and the heavy briefcase he was carrying. The suspicious staff sergeant asked Haeften to whom the briefcase belonged. He was told that it was Stauffenberg's briefcase and that it was needed for the meeting with Hitler.

That meeting in the presence of the Führer was scheduled for 13.00 hours. But Mussolini was due to visit Hitler at 14.30 hours, and to allow preparations to be made for the visit, the meeting was brought forward by half an hour to 12.30 so that the briefing would be finished before the recently deposed Italian dictator arrived. This meant that Stauffenberg then had to hurriedly arm the bomb. He asked Keitel's adjutant, Major Ernst John von Freyend, if there was anywhere he could change his shirt before meeting the Führer, which he told von Freyend was necessary due to seepage from his wounds.

Exactly to which room von Freyend ushered Stauffenberg is unclear. It is variously described as the lounge in Keitel's bunker, the laundry room, which was opposite the room in which Haeften was waiting, and von Freyend's own quarters.[6] Whichever room it was, Stauffenberg entered, being joined by von Haeften (ostensibly to help the one-handed colonel with his change of clothes), who was carrying the second briefcase in which were hidden both bombs.

Stauffenberg had decided to put both bombs into his briefcase to ensure a massive explosion that was certain to kill most, if not everyone, inside. But, before the second one could be transferred, Sergeant Vogel opened the door. Stauffenberg was wanted on the telephone; General der Nachrichtentruppe Fritz Erich Fellgiebel demanded to speak to Stauffenberg on an urgent matter. With the sergeant standing at the door there was only time for Stauffenberg to break the capsule of the chemical timer on one of the bombs with the pair of pliers he had become accustomed to using, with the three fingers of his remaining hand. With the other bomb still in von Haeften's briefcase, Stauffenberg walked out in his fresh shirt to cover the short distance to the brick-encased wooden briefing barracks to meet Hitler himself. A ten-minute timer had been used and in the warmth of late July there was nothing to stop the bomb from exploding. But it was just one bomb containing just 900–1,000g of conventional explosives. Had Fellgiebel, a fellow conspirator, called just a few moments later, Stauffenberg would have had time to arm the second bomb and the consequences of that might indeed have proved fatal to Hitler.

On the walk to what is now Building No. 3, a distance of about 200m, Stauffenberg was joined by General Buhle and von Freyend. Both these men offered to carry Stauffenberg's briefcase for him, but he declined.

The officers attending the meeting were stood chatting at the entrance to the building until Oberst von Below, Hitler's Luftwaffe adjutant, asked them to go in. Shortly afterwards Hitler appeared. The conference room was at one end of the *lagebaracke*. To get to it from the entrance one had to walk along the central corridor past the telephone room and the cloakroom, taking about eight paces to the right and then entering through a double-winged door.[7] Hitler's position was in the centre of the table, where a chair had been placed for the Führer and his polished spectacles laid ready on the table.

Just before entering the hut, Stauffenberg agreed to von Freyend's repeated offer and handed him the briefcase, asking the major to put him as near as

A view along the top of the roof of the remains of the conference barracks. All the windows of the building were covered with steel shutters and shortly after the barracks started to be used for the daily conferences, Hitler ordered the building to be made safe from incendiary bombs. Consequently, the walls on the sides were reinforced with 51cm-thick bricks with an air gap of 15cm all round. The roof was supported by pre-stressed concrete girders.

Such was the weight of the roof, the structure was completely flattened when the *Wolfsschanze* was demolished in 1945.

possible to Hitler so that: 'I catch everything the Führer says for my briefing afterwards.'

In the conference room, which measured about 12m × 5m, Generalleutnant Adolf Heusinger was giving an assessment of the Eastern Front to the assembled officers stood around the room's large rectangular oak table, which, as described earlier, was 6m long and 1.2m wide. It was an uncomfortably hot summer day, no breeze being able to penetrate the trees of the Gorlitz forest. All the windows were open but covered with mesh to keep out the dreaded mosquitoes.

The much-respected Stauffenberg, looked, according to Walter Warlimont, the very model of a General Staff officer: 'The classic image of the warrior through all of history. I barely knew him, but as he stood there, one eye covered by a black patch, a maimed arm in an empty uniform sleeve, standing tall and straight, looking directly at Hitler, who had now also turned round, he was … a proud figure, the very image of the general staff officer.' As Stauffenberg entered the room the Führer shook his hand 'wordlessly, but with his usual scrutinizing look'.

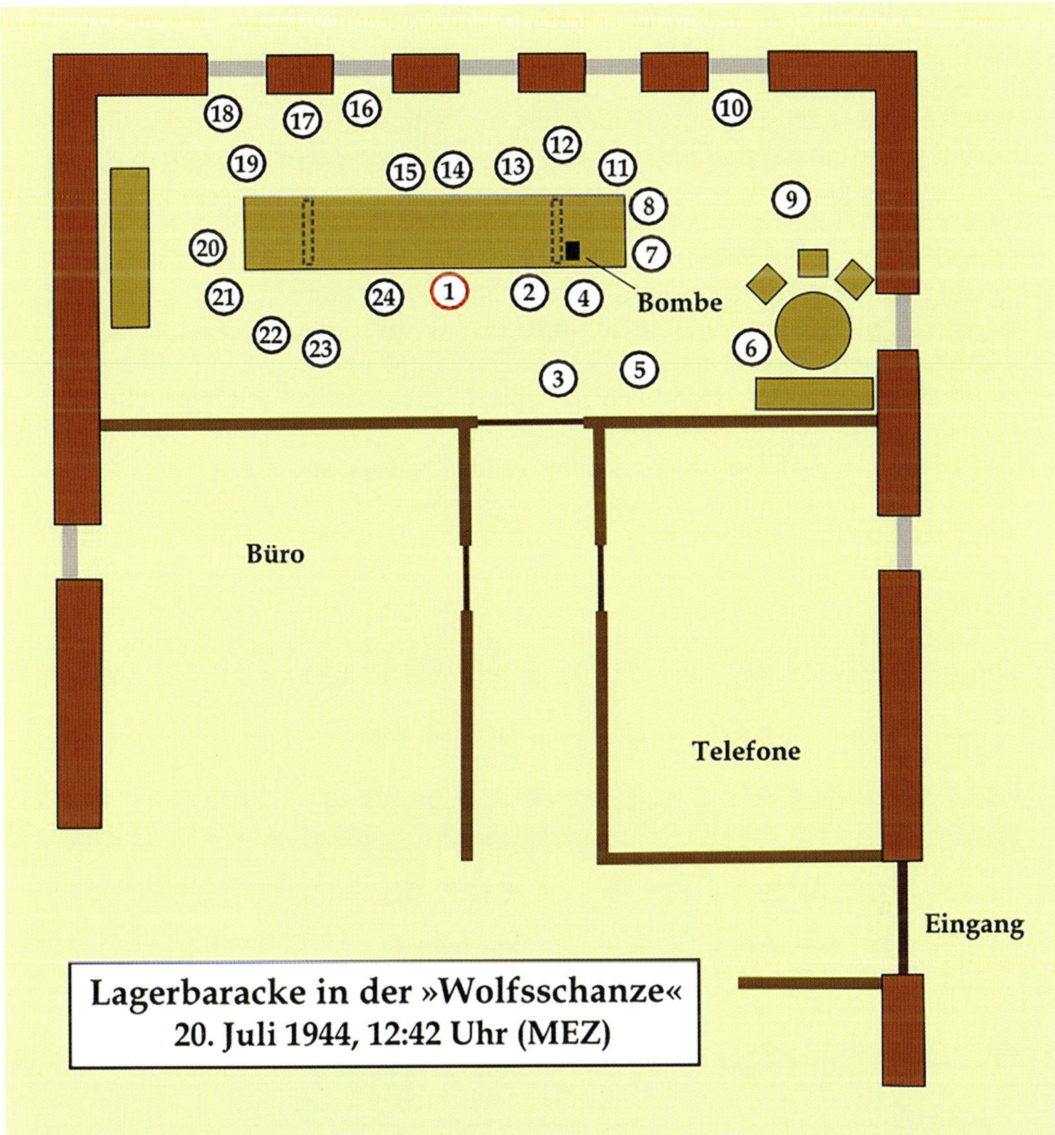

The conference room on 20 July and the approximate positions of those in the building at the time of the explosion: (1) Adolf Hitler, (2) Generalleutnant Adolf Heusinger, (3) Generaloberst Günther Korten, (4) Oberst Heinz Brandt, (5) General der Flieger Karl Bodenschatz, (6) Oberstleutnant Heinz Waizenegger, (7) Generalleutnant Rudolf Schmundt, (8) Oberstleutnant Heinrich Borgmann, (9) General der Infanterie Walther Buhle, (10) Konteradmiral Karl Jesko von Puttkamer, (11) Stenograph Heinrich Berger, (12) Kapitän zur See Heinz Aßmann, (13) Major Ernst John von Freyend, (14) Generalmajor Walter Scherff, (15) Konteradmiral Hans-Erich Voß, (16) SS-Hauptsturmführer Otto Günsche, (17) Oberst Nicolaus von Below, (18) SS-Gruppenführer Hermann Fegelein, (19) Stenograf Heinz Buchholz, (20) Major Herbert Büchs, (21) Ministerialdirigent Franz von Sonnleithner, (22) General der Artillerie Walter Warlimont, (23) Generaloberst Alfred Jodl, (24) Generalfeldmarschall Wilhelm Keitel.

At this point, accounts differ. It is said that Freyend placed the briefcase against one of the table's thick wooded supports near Heusinger and his assistant Colonel Brandt, who were both standing on Hitler's right. Stauffenberg tried to edge closer to Hitler but the only space available was at the corner of the table – and his briefcase remained beyond his immediate grasp and, more significantly, on the opposite side of the wooden support from Hitler.

As Heusinger delivered his inevitably gloomy report, Keitel broke in, suggesting that it would be a good idea to listen to the statement that Stauffenberg was going to give about the fifteen new divisions upon which Hitler placed so much hope, and that Heusinger could continue with his assessment afterwards. But Hitler said he would hear Stauffenberg later and told Heusinger to carry on. Stauffenberg saw that this was his chance to get away, as attention was focused once more on Heusinger and he left the room, whispering to Keitel that he had to take an urgent phone call from Berlin for an update on the numbers available for the Russian front. It was not unusual for men to be going in and out during briefings, and Stauffenberg's departure attracted little attention.

Another version of events is that, upon his arrival, Stauffenberg had slipped his briefcase as close to Hitler as he could, and it was only after he left

Though this photograph was taken in June 1942 at the *Wolfsschanze*, one can imagine that this scene would have been similar to that of 20 July 1944.

A similar meeting in 1943.

the briefing room that Colonel Brandt moved the briefcase behind the right outer wooden table support. Brandt leaned across the table to examine the map more closely and, as he did so, he kicked over Stauffenberg's briefcase. He bent down, picked up the briefcase and, in doing so, moved it behind the wooden support.[8]

There is, however, no divergence of views at what happened next.

Stauffenberg left the Führer Security Zone, passing Kurt Salterberg: 'I had noticed him because of his posture and wounds, especially because of the patch over his right eye, so I took a closer look at the returned day pass and remembered his name, Claus Schenk Graf von Stauffenberg. Now, more strikingly, he came out of the barracks without a belt, without headgear and without the briefcase he had been carrying when he entered.'[9]

Stauffenberg went straight to the signal officer's room in the Wehrmacht adjutant's building where Haeften was waiting. Also there was fellow conspirator Fellgiebel and Oberstleutnant Ludolf Gerhard Sander, one of Fellgiebel's communications officers. But the car that had brought the party from Rastenburg had been driven back to the car parking area. Sander was asked to order a car for Stauffenberg, who said that he had urgent business to conduct.

While waiting for the car to arrive, Stauffenberg heard that Hitler was requesting Stauffenberg's briefing and General Buhle had already set out to find him. The time was 12.40.

Two minutes later, at precisely 12.42 hours, as Hitler stretched out across the table to indicate a point on the large-scale map in front of him, there was a blinding flash followed instantaneously by a deafening roar. Bluish-yellow flame shot out of the windows, hurling with it glass and splinters, and a cloud of choking black smoke. 'In a flash the map room became a scene of stampede and destruction,' recalled Warlimont. 'At one moment ... a set of men ... a focal point of world events; at the next there was nothing but wounded men groaning, the acrid smell of burning; and charred fragments of maps and papers fluttering in the wind. I staggered up and jumped through the open window.'[10]

Stenographer Heinz Buchholz was sitting at the opposite end of the table: 'I remember it as a clap of thunder connected with a bright yellow flash and ever-increasing thick smoke. Glass and wood splintered through the air. The large table on which all the situation maps had been spread out and around which the participants were standing – only we stenographers were sitting – collapsed. After a few seconds of silence ... shouts and screams of pain arose.'[11]

Nicolaus von Below was standing a little to one side discussing the agenda for Mussolini's visit with the other three adjutants: 'Heusinger made a point which interested me, and I moved to the opposite side of the table to obtain a better view of the map. I had been there for a few minutes when the bomb exploded ... I lost consciousness for a few seconds. When I came to I saw around me a ruin of wood and glass. I staggered to my feet, got out through one of the window frames, then sprinted around the hut to the main door. My head was buzzing, I had been deafened and I was bleeding from the head and neck. At the door a terrible scene greeted me. Severely injured officers lay around on the floor, others were reeling around and falling over.'[12]

As the officers who were unwounded came to their senses, their first thought was for Hitler. He had been hurled by the force of the explosion from his original position at the middle of the map table to the vicinity of the left doorpost of the exit: 'Where is the Führer?' Field Marshal Wilhelm Keitel was the first to put into words the thoughts that were running through the minds of the stunned survivors. A figure pulled himself up, covered in dust, his trousers cut to ribbons, his hair on fire – Keitel answered his own question, 'My Führer! You're alive!'[13]

The noise of the explosion caused no alarm in the Wehrmacht adjutant's building, where Sanders commented that animals often triggered mines in the minefield that surrounded the *Wolfsschanze*. The car to take Haeften and Stauffenberg to the airport then arrived and as they climbed in car they saw a body covered by Hitler's cloak being carried from the barracks on a stretcher, and they believed, or chose to believe, that they had killed the Führer. Kurt Salterberger states that, in his opinion, Stauffenberg was too far away from

Hitler was indeed alive despite the devastation caused by the bomb. After his wounds had been dressed and his clothes changed, he returned to the conference room to look at the damage and contemplate his amazing escape.

the *lagebarache* by the time that the bomb went off for him to be able to see clearly any of the casualties.

Stauffenberg told the driver, Leutnant Kretz, to take him back to Rastenburg airfield. The first control post (*Wache* I) was less than 200 yards from the wrecked *lagebarache*, and this was passed without difficulty. Though the barrier was down, Stauffenberg was carrying the correct identification pass and was, anyway, known to the sentry. He allowed the car through, noting in his log: '12.44. Colonel Stauffenberg passed through'. This was only about a minute after the explosion. Salterberg, being much closer to the scene, knew immediately that the explosion had occurred in the conference barracks but even he did not close the exit from the Führer Security Zone until the general alarm had sounded, by which time Stauffenberg was already approaching the last checkpoint.

The sound of the alarm was still reverberating around the *Wolfsschanze*[14] as the conspirators reached the outer control point, where the way to Rastenburg was barred by an anti-tank gun and portable barbed-wire entanglements. The guard, Sergeant Kolbe of the FBB, informed Stauffenberg that as the alarm had been raised, he was not allowed to let anyone pass. There was

Another view of the inside of Building No. 3, the damage being viewed by Göring (third from left) and Bormann on the far left. The destruction in the barrack was considerable.[15]

A photograph showing the extensive damage to the *lagebarache*.

The western exit from the *Wolfsschanze – Wache West* – through which Stauffenberg had to pass to reach the airfield.

Hitler passing the same point at *Wache West* also, presumably, on his way to Rastenburg airfield.

The remains of the support that held the wooden barrier pole at *Wache West* seen raised in the previous photograph to allow Hitler through, as it would have been for Stauffenberg.

no possibility of trying to break through the roadblock, somehow Stauffenberg would have to bluff his way through.

Stauffenberg declared that he had come straight from the Führer with urgent instructions to fly back to Berlin at once. Sergeant Kolbe was unimpressed. The entire conspiracy hung in the balance at this moment.

Stauffenberg entered the guardhouse and telephoned Captain von Möllendorff, the adjutant to the camp commandant, with whom, it may be recalled, he had eaten breakfast that morning. He told Möllendorff: 'I'm in a hurry. General Fromm is waiting for me at the airfield.'[16]

Möllendorff, at that stage of events, had no idea why the alarm had been given and, knowing that Stauffenberg had every right to enter or leave the *Wolfsschanze*, instructed Kolbe to let the car through. As they drove off towards the airfield, Lieutenant Kretz saw Haeften dismantle the second bomb and throw it into the woods. This was later discovered, following a search of the area. It contained 975g of plastic explosives, two initial ignition heads and a British fuse.

The guards at the airfield had not yet been notified of the assassination attempt, and the car passed through unchallenged. Kretz said nothing. By 13.15 hours the two conspirators were in the air and on their way to Berlin.

This is all that remains of the checkpoint manned by Sergeant Kolbe that fateful day.

Once clear of the checkpoints, the second, unused bomb, was thrown out of Stauffenberg's car into the woods. It was later recovered by a team investigating the assassination attempt.

The Guest Bunker in the summer of 1944 around the time it was used by Hitler.

The original paved roadway from the *Wolfsschanze* continues up to Rastenburg airfield.

Rastenburg airfield is still in use.

Key to the overthrow of the existing order in Berlin and elsewhere was the control of information following the death of the Führer. The conspirators needed all contact between the Nazi leaders at the *Wolfsschanze* and the outside world to be blocked long enough for the conspirators to take over the reins of power and arrest the leading SS, Gestapo and Nazi leaders. All communications both to and from the *Wolfsschanze* were handled by Eric Fellgiebel, the Chief of Wehrmacht communications – and also a fellow conspirator.

The difficulty with this was that while there was one main communications bunker at the *Wolfsschanze*, it was not the only one, as Himmler, Ribbentrop and Bormann, who had their own large bunkers within the *Wolfsschanze*, also had their own independent communications set-ups. There were also other means by which information could be passed from the *Wolfsschanze*, including a radio set in Hitler's train. However, set deep within rural East Prussia, the *Wolfsschanze* was a long way from Berlin and there were four repeater stations at Rastenburg, Angerburg, Allenstrin and Lötzen from where signals were transmitted to the Reich capital and beyond. While Fellgiebel clearly could not shut down these four stations by himself, numbers of officers sympathetic to the cause had been placed in the signal stations and all were ready to act as soon as the message was received that Hitler had been assassinated. That it was possible for the conspirators to be able to shut down the Reich's communications in this manner indicated just how widespread the resistance to Hitler had become by this stage of the war.

Waiting for that call to say Hitler had been killed was Fellgiebel's Chief of Staff in Berlin, General Fritz Thiele. At 13.15 hours, his phone rang. It was Fellgiebel: 'Something fearful has happened. The Führer is still alive.' That was all Fellgiebel said and it left Thiele thoroughly confused; this would have a profound effect upon the events that followed. Did Fellgiebel mean that the assassination attempt had not taken place, or did it mean that the attempt had been made but that Hitler had survived?

Thiele immediately informed Fromm's second-in-command, General der Infanterie Friedrich Olbricht, who was standing by to initiate *Valkyrie* on Fromm's authority. Neither man knew what to make of Fellgiebel's cryptic message. So, rather than commit to a course of action from which there was no turning back and, as earlier attempts had been aborted at the last minute, Olbricht decided to do nothing until Stauffenberg returned with some positive information. As a result, vital hours were lost – and with that delay the coup was fatally compromised.

Fellgiebel, unaware of the reaction, or lack of it, to his phone call, assumed that the *Valkyrie* operation had begun and he undertook his part in the plan by contacting his accomplices at the repeater stations, instructing them to block all communications with the *Wolfsschanze* for as long as they could. As it happened, this was not necessary as Hitler demanded that no one should know about the attempt upon his life until more was known, and Sander immediately put this instruction into action. The only people who were to be informed were the leading Nazi officials who were to hunt down the conspirators. Phone calls were made by Sander to Göring, Himmler and Admiral Karl Doenitz, the men being summoned to the *Wolfsschanze*. It was Himmler who was to take charge of the operation.

At first it was thought that the bomb had been laid by some of the foreign construction workers of the Todt Organisation and Speer was worried that he might be blamed. Goebbels, in fact, challenged Speer to state what security checks had been put in place for workers allocated to the *Wolfsschanze*: 'All I could tell him,' Speer explained, 'was that hundreds of workers were admitted into *Sperrkreis* I every day to work on the reinforcement of Hitler's bunker.' He had to admit that under such circumstances it would have been easy for anyone to get into what was supposedly the most carefully secured area in the world.[17]

However, the hurried departure of Stauffenberg and his strange behaviour was soon remarked upon. Stauffenberg had left the briefing to make, or take, a telephone call to Berlin. Yet, according to Wachtmeister Arthur Adam, the telephone operator, Stauffenberg left without making or taking any such call.

He had also left so hurriedly that he left behind his cap and belt, as Salterberg had earlier noted. It very soon became obvious that Stauffenberg was the culprit.[18]

The assassination attempt had failed, but with Hitler and many of the senior Nazis far away in East Prussia, there was still a chance that the coup could succeed. Vital hours had been lost waiting for Stauffenberg to return to Berlin and, astonishingly, even more time was lost because when Stauffenberg and Haeften arrived at Berlin's Rangsdorf airfield at around 15.45 hours, there was no one there to pick them up. A car was eventually sent, but the pair did not reach the Bendlerblock until approximately 16.30 hours.

Though there was absolutely no definitive proof that Hitler had been killed, upon his arrival in the capital, Stauffenberg told the conspirators that Hitler was dead. Though the conspirators then moved into action, too much time had been lost because, at 16.05 hours, communication between the *Wolfsschanze* and the outside world had been restored.

Key to the success of the coup was the issuing of the *Valkyrie* order, which could only be done by General Fromm. If Hitler had been assassinated, then Fromm would not have hesitated to initiate the order. But, by the time that Olbricht approached Fromm to order *Valkyrie*, the general had already been in touch with Keitel at the *Wolfsschanze* to learn that an assassination had been

A photograph taken shortly after the explosion. Hitler has what appears to be a plaster on his left hand and bandaging on a finger of his left hand.

A memorial to Claus von Stauffenberg on the site of Building No. 3, the destroyed conference barracks. The inscription reads in Polish and German: 'Here was the barracks in which Claus Schenk Graf von Stauffenberg attempted an assassination attempt on Adolf Hitler on July 20, 1944. He and many others who rose against the National Socialist dictatorship paid with their lives.'

There are a number of memorials to the assassination attempt at the site of Building No. 3.

attempted and had failed. Fromm told Olbricht that there was, therefore, no need to resort to *Valkyrie*.

Stauffenberg countered by saying that Keitel was bluffing, and he urged his co-conspirators to push ahead with their plans. Fromm still refused to co-operate and was arrested. The *Valkyrie* order was issued under Fromme, but without his authority, and signed by Generalfeldmarschall Erwin von Witzleben, who was officially retired, and Generaloberst Hoepner, who had been dismissed from the Wehrmacht. Though attempts were made to implement these orders, at 18.30 hours, Goebbels delivered a radio broadcast announcing that an attempt had been made on Hitler's life, but the Führer had escaped relatively unharmed. Counter orders were also sent out, some directly from the *Wolfsschanze*, as the coup attempt began to falter. As the evening progressed, it became increasingly evident that the coup had failed and many of its supporters, fearing Hitler's inevitable retribution, began to distance themselves from the still adamant, but increasingly isolated, Stauffenberg.

One man who played an instrumental part in the collapse of the coup attempt now takes centre stage. Major Otto Ernst Remer, in command of the Grossdeutschland Guard Battalion, was not convinced by the orders he had received from the Berlin City Commandant, General Paul von Hase, to cordon off roads into Berlin and to surround important government installations and SS barracks. Deeply troubled by the signatures on the instructions he had received, he sent one of his officers, Lieutenant Hans Hagen, his liaison officer with the Ministry of Propaganda, to check with Goebbels that Hitler was really dead. When Hagen returned with the news that Goebbels had just spoken to a very-much alive Führer on the telephone, Remer knew that he was being complicit in a coup and he reacted swiftly.

Along with a number of SS units, Remer led his battalion to the War Ministry at the Bendlerblock, where they fought their way through the conspirators in a ten-minute gun battle in which Stauffenberg was wounded in his upper left arm, and released Fromm. The conspirators were arrested. Knowing that he had been aware for some time of a plot to kill Hitler but had done nothing about it, Fromm sought to erase the evidence by executing the leading conspirators. 'In the name of the Führer,' he announced, 'a summary court-martial called by myself, has reached the following verdict: Colonel of the General Staff Mertz von Quirnheim, General Olbricht, the Colonel – I cannot bring myself to name him [meaning, of course Stauffenberg] – and Lieutenant von Haeften, are condemned to death.'

The condemned men were taken into the courtyard of the Bendlerblock, where they were shot. This act marked the end of the *Valkyrie* plot, but not the end of the killing. In the subsequent investigation into the conspiracy, some 7,000 people were arrested and 4,980 were executed, including General Fromm.

The thick oak support of the table in the briefing room unquestionably saved Hitler from serious, possibly even fatal, injury. Of the twenty-four people in the room at the time of the explosion, only four subsequently died of their wounds, thanks to that wooden table support and the fact that there was only one bomb in Stauffenberg's briefcase. The fatal or severely injured had all stood to the right of Hitler, on the right half of the table, while all who had suffered only moderate or minor injuries had been on the Führer's left. Those that had worn trousers suffered cuts to their lower legs, while those wearing high leather boots were largely spared such injuries.

Salterberg saw Hitler shortly after he had emerged from the wrecked building: 'Hitler was completely slumped, he did not speak and just stared absent-mindedly ahead. His black pants were completely torn up to the knee. The hands and face were smeared with blood. I couldn't see any other injuries. After the group was a few metres away from the barracks, Adolf Hitler turned around again, stood for a long moment, looked at the building.'

Heinz Linge recalled that fateful day in his memoirs: 'At that time I was about 100 metres away discussing details of the forthcoming Mussolini visit with the head of protocol, von Dörnberg, and other officials. Suddenly there was an explosion. We continued to talk, assuming that Hitler's German shepherd, which had the run of the place, had set off one of the landmines which surrounded FHQ for its security. A few minutes later an orderly came running to our room and cried in a trembling voice: "Hauptsturmführer Linge, go at once to the Führer!" I sensed immediately that something terrible had occurred. As I was running to Hitler's bunker, Major von Freyend, Keitel's adjutant, came up at the trot. He was greatly distressed, blood running down his face. Horrified, I asked what had happened. He gasped: "The Führer is alive and is in the small dining room of the bunker." When I got there Hitler looked at me questioningly with great eyes and noticed my concerned expression. With a calm smile he said: "Linge, someone tried to kill me."

'His uniform was in ribbons. His hair was singed and hung down in strands. My knees were trembling, but he acted as though nothing had happened.'[19]

After Hitler had the splinters from the wrecked table removed from his leg, and his wounds dressed by Dr Hasselbach, Linge helped Hitler put on a new uniform and then went to see the scene of the crime for himself: 'There were still some soldiers outside, groaning. Berger, the stenographer who had been seated opposite Hitler, was dead. The bomb had torn off his legs. The chief of the Luftwaffe General Staff, whose legs had been crushed, was growing close to death. He and Dr Karl Brant, who had been standing next to Hitler and had taken most of the blast, died almost immediately afterwards. Schmundt, who lost an eye and a leg, died two weeks later in the military hospital at Rastenburg.'

Later that day, at around 15.00 hours, Hitler asked his secretary, Christa Schroder, to come and see him. 'As I entered his bunker,' she wrote in her memoirs, 'he rose with some effect and gave me his hand. He looked surprisingly fresh and spoke about the assassination attempt: "The heavy table leg diverted the explosion. The stenotypist sitting near me had both legs blown off. I had extraordinary luck! If the explosion had happened in the bunker and not in the wooden hut, nobody would have survived it. But haven't I always anticipated that happening?"'[20]

As Hitler assessed correctly, the blast from the explosion would have been concentrated had it occurred in Hitler's windowless concrete bunker, but in the wooden hut, its windows open, much of the strength of the blast was dissipated. Damage to the hut itself was considerable: the heavy oak table had collapsed, at least one of the supports and about a fifth of the table top had been shattered. The walls to the east of the aisle, adjacent to the storage room, were torn down, and a hole in one of the wooden floors gaped half a metre wide where the bomb had exploded. The windows and curtains, telephones, lamps, etc. had been damaged or torn to pieces. A number of floorboards had been pushed up as the blast erupted through the floor cavity.[21]

Despite his injuries, Hitler still attended the evening situation meeting at 22.00 hours, which he opened by speaking about the death and injury suffered by those hurt in the explosion. Afterwards, he went to the teahouse,

Hitler with senior Nazi Party officials and Mussolini after the attempted assassination.

where he read out to a gathering of his secretaries, adjutants and some of his officers, a message that he intended to broadcast to the nation. That message, lasting six minutes, which went out at 01.00 hours on 21 July, told the German people of the assassination attempt and finally ended all hope of a coup:

> For the third time an attempt on my life has been planned and carried out. If I speak to you to-day it is, first in order that you should hear my voice and that you should know that I myself am unhurt and well; second, in order that you should know about a crime unparalleled in German history. The claim made by the usurpers that I am no longer alive is being contradicted at this very moment now that I am speaking to you.
>
> The bomb was placed by Colonel Graf von Stauffenberg. A number of colleagues very dear to me were very seriously injured. I myself sustained only some very minor scratches, bruises and burns ... The bombs exploded two metres to my right. One of those with me has died. I myself am completely unhurt.
>
> It has again been granted to me that I should escape a fate which would have been terrible, not for me but for the German people. They see in this again the pointing finger of Providence, that I must and will carry on with my work.[22]

Hitler did indeed carry on, but he had been badly hurt, both physically and psychologically, and he was never quite the same again.

Chapter 9

The End in the East

Hitler was more seriously injured by the assassination attempt than is often appreciated. Though he had more than a hundred oak splinters removed from his legs, mainly his right one, at first it appeared that Hitler had survived the blast surprisingly well. When Morell rushed into Hitler's quarters after hearing the explosion, the Führer remarked: 'It's nothing really.' Then with an actual smile on his face he declared: 'I'm invulnerable. I'm immortal!'

Hitler was also well enough to receive Mussolini on his planned visit, at 15.30 hours. Hitler went to the *bahnhof* to greet the Italian leader, the pair driving back to *Sperrkries* I accompanied on the short journey by armoured vehicles. Hitler took his old friend to the situation barracks to show him the damage done by Stauffenberg's bomb and to revel once again in his remarkable survival.

The two leaders had tea together and when walking down to the tearoom Hitler was determined to show everyone that he was alive and seemingly untroubled by the event, with the Führer making a point of talking to the Todt workers as he passed by them to assure them that they were not under any suspicion. At the meal were Göring, Himmler and Ribbentrop, as well as an interpreter who recorded the following: 'At the beginning of the talk the Duce congratulated the Führer with heartfelt words on his survival of the bomb attempt. The Duce was deeply moved upon hearing the details related to him by the Führer concerning the train of events surrounding the assassination attempt. He interpreted the Führer's escape as a clear indication of the intervention of the Almighty. It was certain that anybody who always miraculously survived the assassination attempts of his enemies must also be led to a victorious finale in the current conflict.'[1]

One of the most remarkable immediate effects of the explosion was that the trembling in his left leg that the increasingly frail Hitler had been suffering from disappeared. However, he had second-degree burns on his calf and two fingers of his left arm. His hair was singed, and he had severe bruising and open flesh wounds.

Other symptoms also manifested themselves, and as the weeks passed by, Hitler's health deteriorated rapidly. His right arm, which had been damaged in the explosion, trembled constantly and his skin and eyes became noticeably jaundiced.

Hitler's survival was indeed remarkable. These are the trousers worn by Luftwaffengeneral Günther Korten, who was mortally wounded, dying two days later. He was stood just two men away from Hitler when the bomb exploded.

Here Hitler is showing Mussolini the extent of the damage to the room where he was stood less than two hours earlier.

Mussolini saying goodbye after his visit on 20 July. In just a few months Hitler himself would be boarding his train to bid his farewell to the *Wolfsschanze*.

He increasingly secluded himself in his quarters, becoming more and more withdrawn. He shuffled around his bunker, and occasionally the Führer Restricted Area, like an old man, due to a wound to his head that caused damage to Hitler's inner ear. This affected his balance. He believed that he was falling to the right and when he was walking outside his bunker at night he would stumble to the right off the path into the darkness. Gradually, the damage to his ear became less pronounced, but then the trembling to his left leg returned.

He was also wracked with stomach cramps, which were so severe that one morning he could not get out of bed, would not eat and showed no interest in the war situation. His stomach pains continued remorselessly. Often, he would struggle to stand upright, suffering severe and painful flatulence. Frau Exner, of course, was no longer there to help him.

Morell believed that the conditions at the *Wolfsschanze* were adding to Hitler's problems: 'I again proposed most urgently a change of air (to Berlin) either for two or three days and then to the mountain for twelve to fourteen days, or just Berlin for eight to ten days,' the doctor wrote in his diary. 'He rejects the Berghof out of hand and says Berlin is unsuitable as he (the patient) would have to keep going down into the bunker, and he cannot walk much at

Admiral Karl Dönitz gave a radio speech at the Wolf's Lair on 21 July, the day after the assassination attempt. Also visible are Hitler himself, Julius Schaub, Martin Bormann, Otto Dietrich and Alfred Jodl (with a bandaged head).

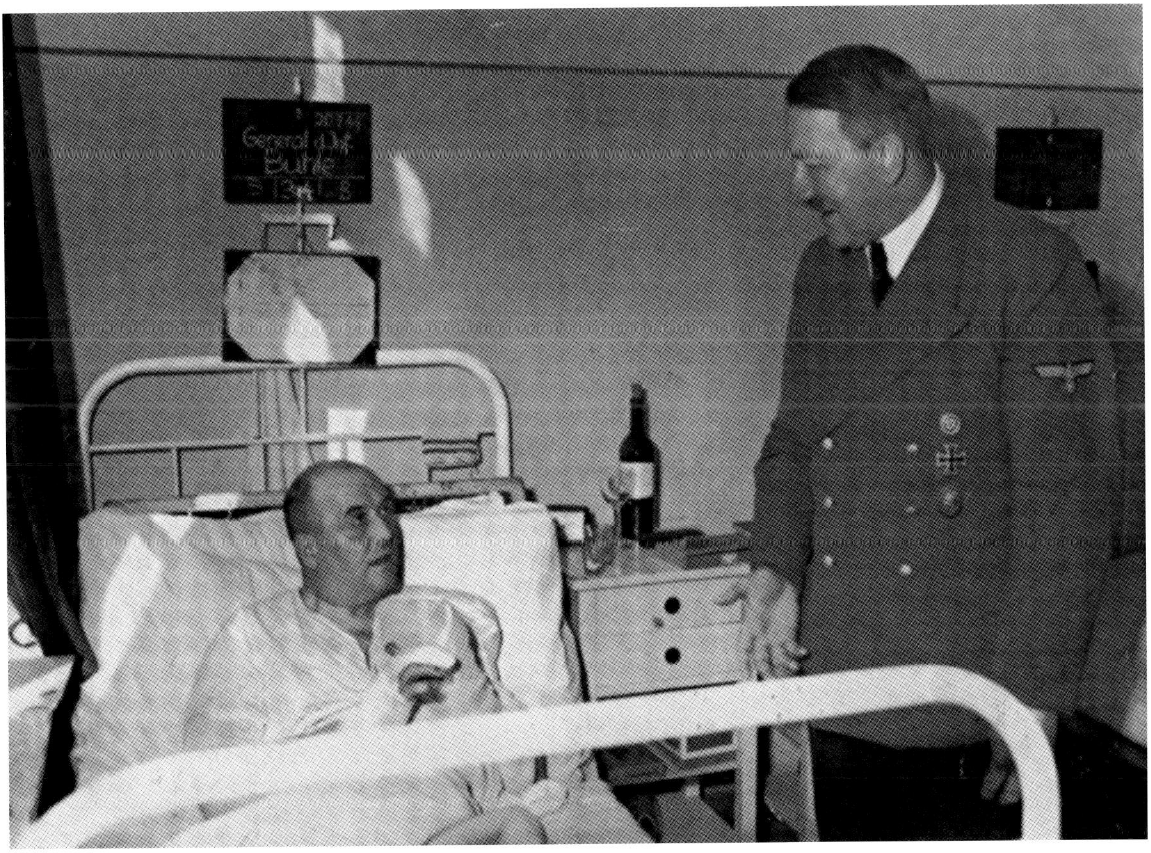

Those who were badly wounded by the bomb were taken to the Carlshof Institutions (*Carlshöfer Anstalten*) near Rastenburg. Hitler went to visit them and here we see him talking to General der Infanterie Walther Buhle. This building was taken over by the SS on 11 February 1941, which used the site as a military hospital and barracks for the SS guards of the *Wolfsschanze*. It was also here that those who were involved in Dr Todt's plane crash were taken. The building now houses the complex of schools of the Agricultural Education Centre in what is today's Karolewo.

present, he is too weak. I referred to the unsuitability of the new bunker for him, the living and sleeping quarters are tiny and despite the ventilation system there is far too little oxygen.'[2]

Martin Bormann was equally concerned about the state of Hitler's health, writing the following to Frau Gerda on 1 October 1944: 'The Führer lives downstairs in his bunker room, has only electric light, and where the air pressure is constantly too high because fresh air has to be pumped in – and it is exactly as if he was living in a basement ... He also nags about our huts with the brick walls that, he says, are destroyed in the first heavy air raid ... I have made myself unwell worrying about the Führer's illness. Finally everything depends on his health! ... the briefing had to be cancelled for the third day in a row today.'[3]

It had also become noticeable to those close to Hitler that the booming voice that had thrilled the thousands at the great rallies of the past was now reduced to whisper. In fact, there was a medical reason for the weakened condition of his voice. Otorhinolaryngologist Dr Carl Otto von Eicken examined Hitler on 16 November and conducted an X-ray on him two days later, which showed a shadowing of the left maxillary sinus and s small polyp (about 20mm) on his vocal chords.

Some of those around him believed that the pressures of the failing war against the Soviets coupled with the shock of almost being killed by Stauffenberg's bomb had finally broken his spirit and they thought Hitler would never recover. The daily situation reports had to be taken to his bunker, being read to him by Admiral Puttkamer, who was also still suffering from the effects of the explosion and had to limp across on crutches from the conference room.

Inevitably, added security measures were put into place immediately after the assassination attempt. On the night of 20/21 July, units of the Liebstandarte SS Adolf Hitler arrived at the *Wolfsschanze*, sealing off *Sperrkreis* I and guarding all the key buildings, causing some resentment among the incumbent RSD and SS personnel. SS guards were also added to every FBB post throughout the site. Understandably, Hitler's faith in the Army was damaged irrevocably and its role in his protection was diminished as that of the SS increased.[4] Nevertheless, the LSSAH left after two weeks as it was clear that its presence was not necessary.

Other security changes included, predictably, searching the briefcases of any person who was likely to be in the presence of the Führer. This led to an alarm when a hand grenade and a bottle of petrol were found in the briefcase of Captain Ötting, Ribbentrop's adjutant. Ötting was, in fact, carrying out a rarely followed rule that dictated personnel carrying top secret papers should have with them the means of destroying those papers to ensure that they did not fall into the hands of the enemy.

While the Todt workers were not in any way involved in the assassination attempt, they were also subjected to heavily increased security measures. They were subjected to almost daily searches and their every move in the compound was monitored by the SS and RSD officers. When being driven to and from the *Wolfsschanze*, the lorries they were transported in were escorted by armoured vehicles and motorcycle combinations with mounted machine guns.

During his periods of illness at the *Wolfsschanze*, Hitler was once again the subject of a failed assassination attempt, although he was completely unaware of it. Doctor Erwin Giesing, chief medical officer of the Luftwaffe and an ear, nose and throat specialist, was called to treat Hitler's ear injuries. This treatment included doses of highly pure cocaine. This he administered in the form of nose and throat dabs, a highly effective surface application. The cocaine was delivered by courier train from Berlin. According to Giesing, he administered the cocaine to Hitler more than fifty times between July and November 1944. Hitler had become profoundly bothered by the noise from the construction work being carried on at the *Wolfsschanze* and the cocaine mitigated the effects of the banging and crashing of the workers.

The procedure was monitored carefully. In the morning, assistant surgeon Karl Brandt took Giesing to a tent behind the guest bunker, where they went through the strict security measures in place since 20 July. Giesing's bags were emptied and every instrument was examined – even the lightbulbs of the otoscope were taken out and screwed back in again. Giesing had to hand over his uniform cap and his dagger, empty out the contents of his trouser and jacket pockets on to the table, and then turn out his pockets. He got only his handkerchief and keys back, and his fountain pen and pencil were returned afterwards. He was then frisked from top to bottom. The cocaine was left out of these rigid controls; it was already inside kept under lock and key by Linge. It was then that the valet performed his part of the ritual, taking the bottle of cocaine out of the drugs cabinet in the orderly room and inviting Giesing to make his examination.[5]

On one of these occasions, on 1 October, after receiving his dose of cocaine, Hitler's eyes fluttered, he turned a deathly white and passed out. At first, Giesing was terrifyingly alarmed that he had given the Führer a fatal overdose. Then, he realised that Linge had left the room and that he was alone with Hitler, and he saw his chance to get rid of the tyrant: 'At that moment,' Giesing wrote in his diary, 'I did not want such a man to exist and exercise the power of life and death in his purely subjective manner.' He plunged the swab he had been using back into the cocaine bottle, knowing that a second dose could be lethal. He began swabbing Hitler's nose when he was startled by Linge, who had walked back into the room and demanded to know how much longer the treatment was going to take.

Giesing said he was just about finished. He left the bunker not knowing if he had killed the Führer. Giesing then excused himself, saying that he had to return to Berlin, ostensibly claiming that he had to check on his office, which had been bombed. He telephoned the *Wolfsschanze* the following day from Berlin and was relieved to learn that Hitler was still very much alive.[6]

As the Soviet forces advanced ever closer, air-raid warnings now sounded almost every day at the *Wolfsschanze*, though each time there was never more than a single aircraft circling over the forest. Air-raid warnings at night were particularly troublesome. All the lights were turned off and the trees hid whatever moonlight there might have been. Everyone had to make their way to one of the heavy bunkers for protection but finding their way in the dark through the trees was far from easy.

Hitler's health also continued to be a cause of concern and many blamed Morell for slowly poisoning the Führer with his cocktail of medicines, but the doctor continued to insist it was the dank, gloomy bunker that Hitler so rarely left that was the cause of his ailments. Yet Hitler insisted that he had to direct the war in the East from the *Wolfsschanze* and on 21 October his personal bunker (Building No. 13) was declared ready for the Führer to move in. It may be recalled that he had been living in the guest bunker since his return to the *Wolfsschanze* on 15 July. However, there were still problems with the air ventilation system, and he did not move into the bunker until midday on 8 November. Conditions in the new bunker were better than the guest bunker, with superior living and sleeping quarters and, at last, a well-functioning air circulating system. Nevertheless, Herman Giesler, Hitler's Munich architect, was unimpressed, calling Hitler's bedroom a 'windowless cell'. He noted that, apart from his simple army cot, there was just a low table piled with papers, a few books and a telephone. It also had a built-in wash-basin and a separate toilet.

Hitler's stay in his new bunker was to be short-lived. In October 1944 Red Army troops reached the eastern border of East Prussia and Hitler finally accepted that he could not remain so close to the front and had to return to Berlin. Even though it was clear the war on the Eastern Front was lost, and that Hitler would never return to the *Wolfsschanze*, development of the site continued, with 2,000 labourers and engineers still working when the Führer departed. As Walter Warlimont remarked, the concrete on the great towers of the *Wolfsschanze* had hardly dried when Hitler left the *Wolfsschanze* on a packed *Brandenburg* for the final time on the morning of 20 November 1944, with the Soviets closing in.

The reason given for his departure was to have the polyp removed from his vocal chords, still declaring that he would return after the minor operation that von Eicken would perform. What he actually told his staff was that he was leaving the *Wolfsschanze* to oversee the Ardennes offensive and that he, and they, would soon be returning to the Wolf's Lair. No one believed it.

Hitler aimed to arrive in Berlin at night to keep his presence in the German capital a secret. 'We left the Wolf's Lair with the rather melancholy feeling of saying a final farewell,' wrote Traudl Junge. 'I had enjoyed life in the forest and had taken the landscape of East Prussia to my heart. Now we were leaving it – for ever.'[7] It was a sorrowful journey for Frau Junge accompanying Hitler: 'His voice scarcely rose above a whisper. His eyes remained rooted to his plate or gazed distantly at a spot on the white tablecloth.'

Hans Baur expressed similar sentiments: 'Those of us from Bavaria had not gone willingly to Rastenburg, but we stayed there three years, and in that time we learned to appreciate the very different countryside of East Prussia and the sterling qualities of its inhabitants, so that in the end it was a real wrench to leave it, for we knew very well that we should not be going back there again.'[8]

Two days later, the decree to destroy the *Wolfsschanze* to prevent it falling into Soviet hands intact – Operation *Inselsprung* – was issued by Keitel. The man in charge of the destruction of the vast complex was Generalleutnant Eduard Hauser, with the actual work being conducted by personnel under the command of General der Pioniere Alfred Jacob. This took place on the night of 24/25 January, and it proved no easy task. It has been estimated that around 8 tons of TNT were used to destroy each of the large bunkers, with huge blocks of concrete being blasted 20m into the air and thrown as far as 60ft away. The shockwaves from the explosions, witnesses claimed, cracked the ice in the nearby Lake Moysee and the tiles were blown off the roofs of some of the houses in the village of Partsch about 2km away. The railway line and associated facilities, which connected all the sites, including the former Görlitz Bahnhof, was also destroyed. All documents left behind were burned.

On 25 January Hauser reported to Fourth Army Command that: 'Preparations for *Inselsprung* completed. Time required 18 hours. *Mauerwald* and *Hochwald* have been demolished and burnt respectively.'[9] This information, as we have seen, was erroneous, as *Mauerwald* was not destroyed. Just two days later, Red Army troops took over the Wolf's Lair without a shot being fired.

After the war, the Soviet authorities began the task of making the area around the *Wolfsschanze* safe by clearing the minefields. This meant securing 72 hectares of forest and 52 hectares of open land. This process lasted until 1955, during which time more than 54,000 landmines were discovered and destroyed.

Also left behind by the Germans were building materials that had not been used in the construction of the *Wolfsschanze* and the local Polish population was able to benefit from this by exporting brick, reinforced steel, panelling, pieces of stone, copper and aluminium wires and stoneware pipes.[10]

Hitler's great eastern headquarters, like the Third Reich, was left in ruins.

Opposite Building No. 4 at the *Wolfsschanze* is a memorial to the Polish Army engineers and sappers who were killed clearing the minefields during the 1950s. The clearance of the mines permitted the complex to be opened to the public and the *Wolfsschanze* now attracts visitors from all over the world.

Notes

Chapter 1: *Führerhauptquartiere Wolfsschanze*

1. Heinrich Hoffmann, *Hitler Was My Friend, The Memoirs of Hitler's Photographer* (Frontline, Barnsley, 2011), pp. 127–8.
2. Ian Baxter, in his excellent *Wolf's Lair, Inside Hitler's East Prussian HQ* (History Press, Stroud, 2009), p. 19, states that the architect and designer Peter Behrens was in charge of the construction team, but this cannot have been the case as Behrens died in Berlin on 27 February 1940.
3. Hans Baur, *I Was Hitler's Pilot* (Frontline, Barnsley, 2013), p. 127; Mark Felton, *Planes, Trains & Automobiles – Transporting the Führer*, http://markfelton.co.uk/publishedbooks/planes-trains-automobiles-transporting-hitler
4. www.bunkierkonewka.eu/historia
5. See the website, www.thirdreichruins.com; Mark Felton, *Guarding Hitler, The Secret World of the Führer* (Pen & Sword, Barnsley, 2014), p. 88.
6. Chris McNab, *Hitler's Fortresses, German Fortifications and Defences 1939–1945* (Osprey, Oxford, 2014), p. 379.
7. http://wolfsschanze.pl
8. Felton, ibid., states that the Soviets were soon aware of the existence of the headquarters and of its purpose. One would assume that the huge undertaking in constructing such a massive structure employing so many workers would have been widely known and it is not unreasonable to suspect that the Soviets did learn of the complex.
9. Quoted in Baxter, p. 121.
10. Traudl Junge with Melissa Muller, *Until the Final Hour: Hitler's Last Secretary* (Phoenix, London, 2004) p. 116.
11. Allen Dulles [ed.], *Great True Spy Stories* (Harper & Row, New York, 1968), p. 28.
12. http://wolfsschanze.pl
13. Ian Baxter, *Hitler's Military Headquarters 1939–1945* (Pen & Sword, Barnsley, 2011), pp. 49–50.
14. Traudl Junge with Melissa Muller, *Until the Final Hour: Hitler's Last Secretary* (Phoenix, London, 2004), p. 36.

Chapter 2: Inside The Lair of the Wolf

1. Walter Warlimont, *Inside Hitler's Headquarters 1939–45* (Weidenfeld and Nicholson, London, 1962), p. 172.
2. Neumäker, Conrad, Woywodt, *Wolfsschanze, Hitlers Machtzentrale im II. Weltkrieg* (Weltbild, Augsburg, 2008), p. 53.
3. Interrogation report, Hauptmann Guam, TNA FO1020/3471.
4. Ian Baxter, *Wolf's Lair*, p. 29 writes of a Polish labourer who left his place of work without permission and took a short cut through what Baxter identifies as Sperrkreis, or 'Security Zone' IV, and was spotted walking through the trees by a guard and shot dead.
5. Peter Hoffmann, *Die Sicherheit des Diktators* (Piper Verlag, Munchen, 1992), pp. 215 & 221.

6. Neumarker, *et al.*, p. 71.
7. Kurt Salterberg, *Als Wachsoldat in der Wolfsschanze: Aus der Sicht eines einfachen jungen Soldaten berichtet der Zeit- und Augenzeuge über die Abläufe* Kindle version (Helios Verlag, 2018).
8. http://wolfsschanze.pl
9. R. Raiber, 'The Führerhauptquartiere', *After the Battle* No. 19, 1977, p. 35.
10. Peter Hoffmann, *Zu Dem Attentat Im Führerhauptquartier 'Wolfsschanze' am 20. Juli 1944* (Vertelijahrshrshefte für Zeitgeschichte, 1964).
11. Ibid., p. 100.
12. Heinz Linge, p. 75.
13. David Irving, *The Secret Diaries of Hitler's Doctor* (Focal Pont, London, 2005), p. 144.
14. Hoffmann, ibid., p. 228.
15. Henrik Eberle & Matthais Uhl, *The Hitler Book, The Secret Report by his Two Closest Aides* (John Murray, London, 2006), p. 92.
16. Heinz Linge, *With Hitler to the End, The Memoirs of Adolf Hitler's Valet* (Frontline Books, Barnsley, 2009), p. 35.
17. Jerzy Szynkowski, *Das Führerhauptquartier Wolfsschanze* (Algraf, Bischofsburg, 2000), pp. 159–61.
18. Seidler & Zeigert, p. 163.
19. Eberle & Uhl, p. 92.
20. Ibid., pp. 151–2.
21. Hugh Trevor-Roper, *Hitler's Table Talk 1941–1944* (Weidenfeld & Nicolson Ltd, London, 1953), p. 340.
22. Irving, ibid.
23. Hoffman, *Hitler's Security*, pp. ix–x.
24. John Kelly, 'Adolf Hitler's food taster tells how she cried with relief at surviving after every meal', *Mirror*, 19 September 2014.
25. Conducător effectively means leader and can be equated with Hitler's title of Führer.
26. Christa Schroeder, *He was My Chief, The Memoirs of Adolf Hitler's Secretary* (Frontline, Barnsley, 2012), p. 88.
27. Nicolaus von Below, *At Hitler's Side, The Memoirs of Hitler's Luftwaffe Adjutant 1937–1945* (Frontline, Barnsley, 2019), p. 106.
28. Baxter, p. 45.
29. Traudl Junge, *Until the Final Hour, Hitler's Last Secretary* (Phoenix, London, 2005), p. 43.
30. Unknown to Hitler, Martin Bormann gave Heim the role of recording Hitler's ideas expressed during these teatime conversations, so that they could be preserved for posterity. These were published in 1980 under the title *Adolf Hitler: Monologe im Führerhauptquartier 1941–1944*, by Werner Jockmann. See Schroeder, pp. 91–4.
31. Quoted in Irving, p. 194.
32. Schroeder, p. 96.
33. Quoted in Baxter, p. 49.
34. www.thirdreichruins.com
35. Speer, p. 419.
36. Peter Hoffman, *Hitler's Security*, xii.
37. Franz W. Seidler & Dieter Zeigert, *Hitler's Secret Headquarters, The Führer's Wartime Bases from the Invasion of France to the Berlin Bunker* (Greenhill, London, 2004), p. 99; Baxter, p. 99.
38. Taken from wolfsschanze.pl
39. Herbert Döhring, *et al.*, *Living With Hitler, Accounts of Hitler's Household Staff* (Greenhill, Barnsley, 2018), p. 33.
40. Major General Walter Dornberger, *V2* (Hurst and Blackett, London, 1954), pp. 101–2.

41. Hitler's adjutant, von Below, and others close to Hitler at the Wolfsschanze denied that Hitler ever watched the film. See John Toland, *Adolf Hitler* (Wordsworth Editions, Ware, 1997), p. 818.
42. Rochus Misch, *Hitler's Last Witness* (Frontline, Barnsley, 2014), p. 86.
43. R. Raiber, *op. cit.*
44. Junge, p. 32.
45. Irving, p. 88.
46. Heinrich Hoffmann, p. 206.
47. Taken from wolfsschanze.pl
48. Seidler & Dieter Zeigert, p. 95.
49. Traudl Junge, p. 36.
50. Irving, p. 80.
51. Ibid.
52. Schroeder, pp. 86–7.
53. Junge, p. 103.
54. Speer, pp. 273–4.
55. Czeslaw Puciato, *Wolfsschanze Plan* (2014).
56. Alexander Stahlberg, *Bounden Duty, The Memoirs of a German Officer 1932–45* (Brassey's London, 1990), pp. 250–1.
57. Hoffmann, *Hitler's Personal Security*, p. 238.
58. Franz W. Seidler & Dieter Zeigert, *Hitler's Secret Headquarters, The Führer's Wartime Bases, from the Invasion of France to the Berlin Bunker* (Greenhill, London, 2004), p. 119.
59. Denis Rigden, *Kill the Führer, Section X and Operation Foxley* (History Press, Stroud, 2009), p. 181.
60. Heinrich Hoffmann, p. 209.
61. Warlimont, p. 438.
62. markfelton.co.uk/publishedbooks/wolfs-lair
63. Baxter, *Wolf's Lair*, p. 27.
64. Quoted in Szynkowski, p. 79.
65. Hoffmann, *Hitler's Personal Security*, pp. 235–6. See also Baxter, *Wolf's Lair*, pp. 141–3, for a full list of weapons and armoured vehicles at the Wolfsschanze in 1944.
66. See Baxter, *Wolf's Lair*, pp. 123–9.
67. B. Plebańczyk, *Mamerki, Przewodnik Turystyczny* (Wydawnictwo, Gdynia), p. 8.
68. Linge, pp. 155–6.
69. Albert Speer, *Inside the Third Reich* (Phoenix, London, 1995), p. 526.

Chapter 3: *Oberkommando des Heeres Mauerwald*

1. Seidler & Zeigert, p. 94.
2. Ferdinand Prinz von der Leyen, Ruckblick zum Mauerwald, Vier Kriegsjahre in OKH (Biederstein Verlag, Munich, 1965), p. 14.
3. http://mazury.info.pl/atrakcje/mamerki
4. Ferdinand Prinz von der Leyden, *Rücklick zum Mauerwald, Vier Kriegsjabre in OKH* (Biederstein Verlag, München, 1965), p. 14.
5. Hans-Georg, www.geschichtsspuren.de
6. Von der Leyen, p. 14.
7. Jerzy Szynkowski, p. 202.

Chapter 4: *Feldkonnandostelle Hochwald*

1. http://mazury.info.pl
2. Baxter, p. 126.
3. Seidler & Dieter Zeigert, p. 95.

Chapter 5: *Oberkommando der Luftwaffe, Robinson*

1. Irving, *Goering*, p. 483.
2. Seidler & Zeigert, p. 94.

Chapter 6: Other Headquarters in East Prussia

1. Seidler & Dieter Zeigert, p. 95.

Chapter 7: *Führerhauptquartier Werwolf*

1. Eberle & Uhl, p. 85.
2. Baxter, *Hitler's Military Headquarters*, p. 73.
3. Matthias Uhl and Henrik Eberle, *The Hitler Book: The Secret Report by His Two Closest Aides* (John Murray, London, 1978), p. 400.
4. Below, p. 151.
5. Schroeder, p. 111.
6. Roger Moorehouse, *Killing Hitler, The Third Reich and the Plots to Kill the Führer* (Vintage, London, 2006), pp. 130–1.
7. Seidler & Zeigert, pp. 114–15.
8. Speer, p. 330.
9. Bohdana Orlyuk, 'Hitler Vinnitsa bunker: Ukraine museum plans draw anger', BBC News, 30 June 2011; Schroeder, p. 112.
10. John Ainsworth-Davis, *The Mountbatten Report, New Edition* (Goldeneye Publishing, London, 2015), p. 292.
11. Baxter, *op. cit.*
12. Felton, *Guarding Hitler*, p. 97.
13. Anthony Beevor, *Stalingrad* (Penguin, London, 2007), p. 80.
14. Stahlberg, p. 311.
15. Felton, *Guarding Hitler*, p. 98; Seidler & Zeigert, p. 112.
16. Warlimont, p. 550.

Chapter 8: *Valkyrie* – The 20 July 1944 Assassination Attempt on Hitler

1. Hermann Graml, Hans Mommsen, Hans-Joachim Reichhardt and Ernst Wolf, *The German Resistance to Hitler* (Batsford, London, 1970), pp. 5–6.
2. Hoffmann, p. 327.
3. See Martin Middlebrook and Chris Everitt, *Bomber Command War Diaries: An Operational Reference Book* (Pen & Sword, Barnsley, 2014).
4. https://forum.axishistory.com/viewtopic.php?f=5&t=111316&p=980237; Fest, pp. 224–5.
5. Jones, p. 186.
6. Hoffmann, *Zu Dem Attentat Im Führerhauptquartier 'Wolfsschanze' am 20. Juli 1944*; Jones, p. 187.
7. Eberhard Zeller, *The Flame of Freedom, The German Struggle Against Hitler* (Westview Press, Oxford, 1994), p. 203.
8. Nigel Jones, *Countdown to Valkyrie, The July Plot to Assassinate Hitler* (Frontline, Barnsley, 2008), p. 189.
9. Kurt Salterberg, *op. cit.*
10. Walter Warlimont, *Inside Hitler's Headquarters* (Weidenfeld & Nicolson, London, 1964), p. 440.
11. Quoted in Irving, p. 145.
12. Below, p. 209.
13. Jones, p. 192.

14. Kurt Salterberg, *op. cit.*, states that this was the first time that the alarm had been sounded at the *Wolfsschanze*.
15. Peter Hoffman, *Zu Dem Attentat Im Führerhauptquartier 'Wolfsschanze' am 20. Juli 1944* (Vertelijahrshrshefte für Zeitgeschichte, 1964), pp. 273–4.
16. Michael Thomsett, *The German Opposition to Hitler: The Resistance, the Underground, and Assassination Plots, 1938–1945* (Crux, 2016), p. 174.
17. Speer, p. 513.
18. Adam was rewarded for coming forward with this information, being promoted to was promoted to Oberwachtmeister, and being given 20,000 Reichsmark and a small cottage near Berlin; Wolfgang Malanowski, 'Mein Führer, Sie leben, Sie leben.', *Spiegel Online*, 09.07.1984.
19. Linge, pp. 156–7.
20. Schroeder, p. 122.
21. Hoffmann, Zu Dem Attentat Im Führerhauptquartier 'Wolfsschanze' am 20. Juli.
22. *Guardian*, Friday, 21 July 1944.

Chapter 9: The End in the East

1. Seidler & Zeigert, p. 174.
2. Irving, pp. 167–8.
3. Szynkowski, *Wolfsschanze*, pp. 44–5.
4. Felton, *Guarding Hitler*, p. 129; Peter Hoffman, *Hitler's Personal Security*, p. 253.
5. Norman Ohler, 'Hitler's Doctor Said the Dictator Almost Died from a Cocaine Overdose', *Vice* magazine, 27 March 2017.
6. Toland, pp. 827–8.
7. Junge, p. 146.
8. Baur, p. 167.
9. Hoffmann, *Security*, p. xii.
10. http://wolfsschanze.pl

Sources

Image Credits

All present day photographs are by the author and all period photographs are courtesy of Historic Military Press except where specified below:

Honza Groh, pp. **8**, **9**, **10**, **127**; Fotonews, **10**; flickr/zelerek, **11**, **12**, **13**; wolfsschanze.pl, **18**; Frontline Books, **23**; Bundesarchiv, **28**, **71**, **93**, **162**; Notstromzentrale, **37**; Narodowe Archiwum Cyfrowe, **46**, **272**, **273**, **284**, Federal archives, **99**; Third Reich in Ruins, **107**, **108**; heizhaus, **116**; Mariusz Switulski/Shutterstock, **163**, **164**, **188**, **209**, **237**; Eryk Stawinski/Shutterstock, **237**; Janusz Lipinski/Shutterstock, **239**; Laima Gutmane, **239**; UA-Lora, **242**, **245**, **248**; Håkan Henriksson, **248**; Kabakova Tetiana/Shutterstock, **249**; Ronedya/Shutterstock, **249**; Memnon335bc, **271**.

The National Archive, Kew

FO 1020/3471, Interrogation report, Hauptmann Guam, 3rd Panzer Grenadier Battalion, Führer-Begleit-Brigade.

Books

Ainsworth-Davis, John, *The Mountbatten Report, New Edition* (Goldeneye, London, 2015).

Baur, Hans, *I Was Hitler's Pilot* (Frontline, Barnsley, 2013).

Baxter, Ian, *Wolf's Lair, Inside Hitler's East Prussian HQ* (History Press, Stroud, 2009).

Baxter, Ian, *Hitler's Military Headquarters 1939–1945: Rare Photographs from Wartime Archives* (Pen & Sword, Barnsley, 2011).

Beevor, Anthony, *Stalingrad* (Penguin, London, 2007).

Below, Nicolaus von, *At Hitler's Side, The Memoirs of Hitler's Luftwaffe Adjutant 1937–1945* (Frontline, Barnsley, 2019), p. 209.

Berthold, Will, *Die 42 Attentate auf Adolf Hitler* (Ueberreuter, Wein, 1997).

Döhring, Herbert, Karl, Wilhelm Krause & Plain, Anna, *Living With Hitler, Accounts of Hitler's Household Staff* (Greenhill, Barnsley, 2018).

Dornberger, Major General Walter, *V2* (Hurst and Blackett, London, 1954).

Duffy, James P., & Ricci, Vincent L., *Target Hitler, The Plots to Kill Adolf Hitler* (Praeger, London, 1992).

Dulles, Allen, [ed.], *Great True Spy Stories* (Harper & Row, New York, 1968).

Eberle, Henrik & Uhl, Matthais, *The Hitler Book, The Secret Report by his Two Closest Aides* (John Murray, London, 2006).

Felton, Mark, *Guarding Hitler, The Secret World of the Führer* (Pen & Sword, Barnsley, 2014).

Fest, Joachim, *Plotting Hitler's Death: The German Resistance To Hitler, 1933–1945* (Phoenix, London, 1997).

Graml, Hermann, Mommsen, Hans, Reichhardt, Hans-Joachim, and Wolf, Ernst, *The German Resistance to Hitler* (Batsford, London, 1970).

Hoffmann, Heinrich, *Hitler Was My Friend, The Memoirs of Hitler's Photographer* (Frontline, Barnsley, 2011).

Hoffmann, Peter, *Die Sicherheit des Diktators* (Piper Verlag, Munchen, 1892).
Hoffmann, Peter, *Hitler's Personal Security, Protecting the Führer, 1921–1945* (Da Capo, 2000).
Irving, David, *Goering, A Biography* (Macmillan, London, 1989).
Irving, David, *The Secret Diaries of Hitler's Doctor* (Focal Pont, London, 2005).
Junge, Traudl, with Muller, Melissa, *Until the Final Hour: Hitler's Last Secretary* (Phoenix, London, 2004).
Jockmann, Werner & Heim Heinrich von, *Adolf Hitler: Monologe im Führerhauptquartier 1941–1944*, (Orbis, 2000).
Leyen, Ferdinand Prinz von der, *Ruckblick zum Mauerwald, Vier Kriegsjahre in OKH* (Biederstein Verlag, Munich, 1965).
Linge, Heinz, *With Hitler to the End, The Memoirs of Adolf Hitler's Valet* (Frontline Books, Barnsley, 2009).
Jones, Nigel, *Countdown to Valkyrie, The July Plot to Assassinate Hitler* (Frontline, Barnsley, 2008).
Korpalski, Edward, Szynkowski, Jerzy, Wagner, Heinz, *Wolfsschanze, und das Attentat vom 20. Juli 1944* (Algraf, Biskupiec, Bischofsburg, 2016).
McNab, Chris, *Hitler's Fortresses, German Fortifications and Defences 1939–1945* (Osprey, Oxford, 2014).
Middlebrook, Martin and Everitt, Chris, *Bomber Command War Diaries: An Operational Reference Book* (Pen & Sword, Barnsley, 2014).
Misch, Rochus, *Hitler's Last Witness: The Memoirs of Hitler's Bodyguard* (Frontline, Barnsley, 2014).
Moorehouse, Roger, *Killing Hitler, The Third Reich and the Plots to Kill the Führer* (Vintage, London, 2006).
Neumäker, Uwe, Conrad, Robert, Woywodt, Cord, *Wolfsschanze, Hitlers Machtzentrale im II. Weltkrieg* (Weltbild, Augsburg, 2008).
Plebańczyk, B., *Mamerki, Przewodnik Turystyczny* (Wydawnictwo, Gdynia).
Puciato, Czeslaw, *Wolfsschanze, Tourist Guide* (Bartograf Bartoszyce, Ketrzyz, 1997).
Rigden, Denis, *Kill the Führer, Section X and Operation Foxley* (History Press, Stroud, 2009).
Salterberg, Kurt, *Als Wachsoldat in der Wolfsschanze: Aus der Sicht eines einfachen jungen Soldaten berichtet der Zeit- und Augenzeuge über die Abläufe* (Kindle version, Helios, 2018).
Schroeder, Christa, *He was My Chief, The Memoirs of Adolf Hitler's Secretary* (Frontline, Barnsley, 2012).
Schulz, Alfons *Drei Jahre in der nachrichtenzentrale des Führerhauptquartiers* (Christiana, Berlin, 1997).
Seidler, Franz W., & Zeigert, Dieter, *Hitler's Secret Headquarters, The Führer's Wartime Bases from the Invasion of France to the Berlin Bunker* (Greenhill, London, 2004).
Speer, Albert, *Inside the Third Reich* (Phoenix, London, 1995).
Stahlberg, Alexander, *Bounden Duty, The Memoirs of a German Officer 1932–45* (Brassey's London, 1990).
Szynkowski, Jerzy, *Wolfsschanze. Das Führerhauptquartier: Umfassende Darstellung. Umfangreiches Bildmaterial. Erinnerungen von Zeitzeugen* (Algraf, Bischofsburg, 2000).
Szynkowski, Jerzy, *Hitler's Kriegsquartiere Kurzinformationen* (Kengraf, 2002).
Thomsett, Michael, *The German Opposition to Hitler: The Resistance, the Underground, and Assassination Plots, 1938–1945* (Crux, 2016).
Toland, John, *Adolf Hitler* (Wordsworth Editions, Ware, 1997).
Trevor-Roper, Hugh, *Hitler's Table Talk 1941–1944* (Weidenfeld & Nicolson Ltd, London, 1953).
Warlimont, Walter, *Inside Hitler's Headquarters 1939–45* (Weidenfeld and Nicholson, London, 1962).
Zeller, Eberhard, *The Flame of Freedom, The German Struggle Against Hitler* (Westview Press, Oxford, 1994).

Online

BBC News
bunkierkonewka.eu/historia
Felton, Mark, *Planes, Trains & Automobiles – Transporting the Führer*,
forum.axishistory.com
Hans-Georg, www.geschichtsspuren.de
Hoffmann, Peter, *Zu Dem Attentat Im Führerhauptquartier 'Wolfsschanze' am 20. Juli 1944* (Vertelijahrshrshefte für Zeitgeschichte, 1964)
mazury.info.pl/atrakcje/mamerki
thirdreichruins.com
wolfsschanze.pl

Pamphlets, Newspapers and Periodicals

Kelly, John 'Adolf Hitler's food taster tells how she cried with relief at surviving after every meal', *Mirror*, 19 September 2014.
Puciato, Czeslaw, *Wolfschanze Plan* (2014).
Raiber, R., 'The Führerhauptquartiere', *After the Battle*, No. 19 (1977), p. 35.
Spiegel Online.
Vice magazine, March 2017.